P9-EDZ-122

Television

OTHER TITLES IN THE TECHNOLOGY 360 SERIES:

Cell Phones
Global Positioning Systems
iPod and MP3 Players
Online Social Networks
Robots
Video Games
Web 2.0

HNOLOGY 360

Television

John Grabowski

LUCENT BOOKS
A part of Gale, Cengage Learning

GALE
CENGAGE Learning™

Detroit • New York • San Francisco • New Haven, Conn • Waterville, Maine • London

© 2011 Gale, Cengage Learning

LIBRARY OF CONGRESS CATALOGING-IN-PUBLICATION DATA

Grabowski, John.
    Television / by John Grabowski.
        p. cm. — (Technology 360)
    Includes bibliographical references and index.
    ISBN 978-1-4205-0169-8 (hardcover)
    1. Television—Juvenile literature. I. Title.
    TK6640.G66 2011
    621.388--dc22
                                        2010033525

Lucent Books
27500 Drake Rd
Farmington Hills MI 48331

ISBN-13: 978-1-4205-0169-8
ISBN-10: 1-4205-0169-0

Printed in the United States of America
1 2 3 4 5 6 7 15 14 13 12 11
Printed by Bang Printing, Brainerd, MN, 1st Ptg., 02/2011

CONTENTS

Foreword   6
Important Dates in the Development of Television   8

Introduction
A Modern Miracle   10

Chapter 1
Inventing the Technology   16

Chapter 2
The Networks Take Control   33

Chapter 3
A Variety of Choices   53

Chapter 4
Improving the Product   68

Chapter 5
Into the Future   86

Notes   100
Glossary   104
For More Information   105
Index   106
Picture Credits   111
About the Author   112

FOREWORD

As we go forward, I hope we're going to continue to use technology to make really big differences in how people live and work.
—Sergey Brin, cofounder of Google

The past few decades have seen some amazing advances in technology. Many of these changes have had a direct and measurable impact on the way people live, work, and play. Communication tools, such as cell phones, satellites, and the Internet, allow people to keep in constant contact across longer distances and from the most remote places. In the medical field, existing technologies, such as digital imaging devices, robotics, and lasers, are being used to redefine surgical procedures and diagnostic techniques. As technology becomes more complex, the related ethical, legal, and safety issues become more complex as well.

Psychologist B.F. Skinner once noted that "the real problem is not whether machines think but whether men do." Recent advances in technology have drastically changed the way people view the world around them. They can have a phone conversation with someone located thousands of miles away, access a huge amount of information using a computer, or become an avatar in a virtual world of their own making. A closer examination of the evolution and use of technological advances provides a deeper understanding of the social, cultural, and ethical implications that they may hold for our future.

The Lucent Books' Technology 360 series not only explores how evolving technologies work, but also examines the short- and long-term impact of their use on society as a whole. Each volume in Technology 360 focuses on a particular invention, device, or family of similar devices, exploring how the device was developed, how it works, its impact on society, and its possible future uses. Volumes also contain a time line specific to each topic, a glossary of terms used in the text, and a subject index. Sidebars, photos, detailed illustrations, tables, charts, and graphs help further illuminate the text.

Titles in this series feature inventions and devices familiar to most readers, such as robots, digital cameras, iPods, and video games. Not only do these titles provide an overview of these inventions, but they also address how much these devices have evolved. For example, in 1973 a Motorola cell phone weighed about 2 pounds (0.9kg) and cost four thousand dollars. Today cell phones weigh only a few ounces and are often offered for free with a cell-phone service contract. Lasers—long a staple of the industrial world—have become highly effective surgical tools, capable of reshaping the cornea of the eye and cleaning clogged arteries. Early video games were played on large machines in arcades; today games are played on sophisticated home systems that allow for multiple players and cross-location networking.

1897

German scientist Karl Ferdinand Braun develops the first cathode ray tube.

1900

Russian scientist Constantin Perskyi becomes the first person to use the word "television," doing so in a paper presented at the Paris World Exhibition.

1921

Fourteen-year-old Philo T. Farnsworth has a vision of an all-electronic television system while plowing the fields at his family's farm.

1941

The National Television Standards Committee (NTSC) announces technical standards for black-and-white television.

1939

Television is introduced to the public at the New York World's Fair. RCA begins selling its first television sets to the public.

1890

1910

1930

1884

German scientist Paul Nipkow invents a device, called an electric telescope, that uses an optical scanning disk to send images over wires.

1928

The Federal Radio Commission issues the first television station license to Charles Jenkins.

1930

David Sarnoff becomes president of the Radio Corporation of America.

in the Development of Television

1948 The first cable television systems bring improved television reception to rural areas of the country.

1953

The National Association of Broadcasters (NAB) adopts its Code of Practices for Television Broadcasters.

1995

Internet television and radio begin.

1956

Zenith begins producing Robert Adler's "Space Command" remote control.

1962

The Telstar communications satellite is launched into orbit.

2009

The analog to digital transition goes into effect on July 12.

1950

1980

2010

1951

The National Association of Broadcasters (NAB) adopts its Code of Practices for Television Broadcasters.

1994

The FCC adopts technical standards for high definition television in the United States.

1956

The Ampex Corporation demonstrates videotape recorder technology.

1976 The first videocassette recorders (VCRs) for home use are introduced.

A Modern Miracle

When the Radio Corporation of America (RCA) introduced America's first consumer television set at the New York World's Fair in 1939, not everyone was convinced of its potential as a form of communication or entertainment. In an editorial that year, the *New York Times* said, "TV will never be a serious competitor for radio because people must sit and keep their eyes glued on a screen—the average American family hasn't time for it."[1]

The *Times*, obviously, misjudged the American public. People made time for it. According to a recent Nielsen survey, Americans now watch television an average of five hours a day. Most Americans depend on the medium for providing them with entertainment and information. Over the past sixty or so years, it has been a powerful cultural force in the lives of millions of people. In that time, there have been numerous changes in the medium's technology and content.

A Changing Technology

Those first fuzzy, black-and-white images of early 1950s televisions have given way to incredibly sharp, clear, high-definition color images that are so lifelike they appear three-dimensional.

Tiny screens that measured only a few inches across, contained in large cabinets that held the machinery and components required to make it work, have evolved into massive screens that can occupy an entire wall while being as thin as a paperback book. Sound systems have also evolved to complement the superior picture quality. Surround sound

Television has changed greatly since the early black and white images of the 1950s to the high-definition color images of today.

systems with high-quality speakers allow viewers to have a movie-theater experience in their own homes.

A Wide Range of Content

Content available for viewing has also undergone a dramatic change. Just a half century ago, families gathered around their television sets and made their selections from a handful

Satellite TV, DVRs, and on-demand services allow viewers more choices than ever before.

of choices delivered primarily over the three major networks: the National Broadcasting Company (NBC), the Columbia Broadcasting System (CBS), and the American Broadcasting Company (ABC). Now, thanks to cable and satellite TV, viewers have literally hundreds of channels from which to choose. Movies, music, sports, news, drama, comedy, education, and even shopping all have their place in today's television lineup. Pay-per-view (PPV) options bring even more live events and feature films into homes. Together with on-demand television and digital video recording (DVR), viewers have in effect become programmers, watching their selections whenever they desire, day or night, rather than at predetermined times.

For those who wish to watch programs while away from home, advances in technology allow them to be viewed on personal computers, cell phones, and portable media players such as an iPod. Prices for these devices continue to drop. It is now possible to watch an episode of one's favorite TV show at a coffee shop, while traveling, or during a lunch break.

A Blessing or a Curse?

There is no denying that television can be informative. Many people get their news by watching television rather than by reading a newspaper. Reading about an event or hearing about it on the radio is much different from actually seeing it as it happens. One example is the terrorist attack on the World Trade Center in New York on September 11, 2001. Events of that day were broadcast live on televisions around the world. Television viewers watched as United Airlines Flight 175 crashed into the World Trade Center's south tower and as thousands of people evacuated New York City on foot as plumes of smoke billowed into the sky. They witnessed the terrifying collapse of each of the center's two towers as they happened. Viewers were horrified by what they saw, and they will never forget it.

Television also provides a wealth of educational programs that take viewers from the bottom of the sea to the farthest reaches of outer space. Similarly, there are programs that provide cooking lessons, offer fitness workouts, or guide viewers through home improvement projects.

Regardless of the variety of programming, television still has its fair share of critics. As the late comedian Groucho Marx once said, "I find television to be very educating. Every time somebody turns on the set, I go in the other room and read a book."[2] Television is a commercial enterprise. The programs that are the most popular with viewers are the ones that attract the most advertisers and make the most money. If violence or tasteless entertainment is what people want to see, then television will give it to them.

The relationship between what humans see and what they do is very complex. Several studies have identified an association between watching violence on television and in movies and violent behavior. Such issues are a concern for everyone, particularly parents of young, impressionable children.

This connection is not the only negative associated with the medium. Some critics are concerned about how much time people spend watching television. Television viewing habits are blamed for rising rates of obesity and the decline in physical fitness. Others argue that it lowers academic performance in school, promotes gender-role and racial stereotypes, and encourages materialistic attitudes due to the commercials. Some people even blame television for the breakdown of the family unit.

Television and Its Effect on the World

Whether television is a blessing or curse will continue to be debated. What cannot be questioned is that it has had a profound effect on people and cultures. In his 1964 book, *Understanding Media*, Canadian professor Marshall McLuhan proposes the theory that a medium affects society more than the content it delivers. Such has certainly been the case with television. Much television programming does not require any intellectual work on the part of the viewer, such as reading or interpreting. Viewers can just sit back and be entertained. Television provides access to events all around the world. At the same time, however, it has lessened communication between members of families.

Television can both entertain and enlighten. It is an important part of people's everyday lives, and its effect on American culture is undeniable. No one knows what the future will bring, but it is certain that television in its various forms is here to stay. As author Paddy Chayefsky once said, "it's the menace that everyone loves to hate but can't seem to live without."[3]

CHAPTER 1

Inventing the Technology

Russian scientist Constantin Perskyi is credited as being the first person to use the word *television*. He did so in a paper he presented at the Paris World Exhibition's First International Congress of Electricity in 1900. Perskyi used the term in reference to the work of the early experimenters in the field. He could not possibly have envisioned the extent to which television has become a part of people's lives.

Television is an invention that touches the life of practically every single American, often for hours at a time, every single day of his or her life. Unlike other inventions, such as the electric light, telephone, and airplane, credit for the invention of television cannot be attributed to one person. Rather, television evolved from the work of numerous people dating back to the nineteenth century.

The Transmission of Sound

The invention of television, by which moving images and sounds are transmitted over great distances, would not have been possible without the contributions of Samuel Morse. In 1838 Morse gave the first public demonstration of his telegraph, which allowed people to send a series of sounds like

beeps or clicks over electrical wires. When decoded, these sounds conveyed a message. The first telegraph line was officially opened on May 24, 1844, and Morse sent the message, "What hath God wrought?" from Baltimore, Maryland, to Washington, D.C.

The telegraph remained the fastest method of long-distance communication until 1876 when the human voice was first transmitted over electrical wires by Alexander Graham Bell. Bell's "electrical speech machine," better known as the telephone, gave individuals the ability to speak to one another over great distances by means of handsets connected to wires.

The next major advance in the field of communications came in 1887. That year, German physicist Heinrich Hertz confirmed the existence of radio waves. Basing his work on a theory proposed by Scottish physicist James Clerk Maxwell some years earlier, Hertz created electromagnetic waves and then transmitted them through the air. He did not, however, realize the importance of his discovery. "This is just

Guglielmo Marconi was the first to send telegraph messages through the air using electromagnetic waves rather than over wire.

an experiment that proves Maestro Maxwell was right," said Hertz. "We have these mysterious electromagnetic waves that we cannot see with the naked eye; but they are there . . . I do not think that the wireless waves I have discovered will have any practical application."[4]

It was Italian inventor Guglielmo Marconi who saw the possibilities in Hertz's work. He came up with a way to send telegraph messages through the air using electromagnetic waves rather than over wires. He sent and received his first signal in 1895. Marconi's work eventually led to the invention of radio, by which voices and music could also be transmitted many miles through the air. Adding moving pictures to radio would eventually form the foundation of television.

American Lee De Forest improved on the new technology with his invention of the Audion vacuum tube in 1906. The Audion amplified signals so that they could be transmitted over greater distances. In 1908 he broadcast a message from the top of the Eiffel Tower in Paris, France. Radio receivers

George R. Carey

By profession, George R. Carey was a surveyor employed by the city of Boston, Massachusetts. He was also an inventor who was one of the first to propose using a selenium camera for telegraphy, or transmitting images over distances by means of electricity.

Carey's camera design called for a metal plate filled with pieces of selenium that were connected to light bulbs in a panel. Light from the object to be photographed entered the camera, where the selenium converted it into electrical signals that were sent to the light bulbs. The bulbs lit up in a pattern that recreated the image.

Carey's camera, which he claimed to have designed in 1877, was never built since it would have been very bulky and expensive to produce. It is still considered a forerunner of both the television and fax machine.

500 miles (805km) away picked up his words. Although De Forest imagined it would be possible to transmit images in this manner in the future, he was not convinced of its practicality. "While theoretically and technically, television may be feasible," he said, "commercially and financially I consider it an impossibility, a development of which we need waste little time dreaming."[5]

Transmitting Images

While Morse, Bell, Marconi, and De Forest were working to transmit sounds, other scientists became consumed with the challenge of transmitting images. Most saw this as the next plausible step following the transmission of sounds. Few, if any, however, imagined how the technology would be used in the future.

Early attempts at what was called "distance vision" focused on the use of the element selenium, which had been discovered by Swedish chemist Jöns Jakob Berzelius in 1817. In 1882 Joseph May, a young Irish telegraph operator, made an important discovery. While working for England's Telegraph Construction and Maintenance Company at its station in Valentia, May was using selenium rods as electrical resistors while maintaining the transatlantic undersea telegraph cable to America. One day he noticed that the rods were reporting varying measurements of resistance when they should have been constant. He eventually realized that these changes occurred when a shaft of sunlight from a nearby window fell on the rods. Since the selenium was responding to differences in light intensity, it suggested that light waves could be converted into electrical impulses that could then be transmitted.

Two years later, German engineering student Paul Nipkow found a way to apply May's discovery to transmit images.

Nipkow Disks

Nipkow created a device that consisted of a rotating disk with a series of eighteen small rectangular holes arranged in a spiral. A beam of light was aimed through the holes at an image. The light illuminated the image one line at a time.

The light beam was converted into an electrical signal by selenium cells. The intensity of the signal was dependent on the darkness of the pieces or elements of the image. The signal was then sent to a receiver where a similar disk reversed the process, turning the signal back into light. The entire image was scanned sequentially in one rotation of the disk. If the disk rotated fast enough, the scanned elements were perceived as a single image. The reason for this is because when an image reaches the human eye, it is kept by the retina for approximately one-tenth of a second. If another image replaces the first within that time span, the second becomes superimposed on the first. The two merged images convey an illusion of motion to the brain. This is known as persistence of vision.

Unfortunately the technology of the day was not advanced enough to make the device—which Nipkow called an electric telescope—practical. The selenium did not react to light quickly enough, and the size of the image could not be magnified. Other attempts to solve the problems using mirrors followed, but with limited success. Nipkow's invention, however, laid the foundation for the mechanical television systems that were to follow. They became a reality approximately forty years later. Interestingly two inventors developed mechanical television systems, each without knowledge of the other.

John Logie Baird

John Logie Baird was a Scottish entrepreneur and inventor with a wide range of interests and a fertile imagination. He started a jam-making business on the Caribbean island of Trinidad and developed a thermal undersock to protect the feet in cold weather, a "revolutionary" soap, and a glass razor. John Trenouth, senior curator of television at the National Media Museum in Bradford, North Yorkshire, England, says, "Baird was not a scientist in the strict sense of the word. He had a lot of ideas, and he could sketch out what he wanted—even on tablecloths in restaurants, where they had to put the cloth on the bill so he could take it away with him!"[6]

John Logie Baird's "televisor" from the 1930s, pictured, built upon Paul Nipkow's invention, the Nipkow Disk, from 1884.

Baird's first love was electronics. By the early 1920s, he was concentrating his talents on developing a television system. The response time of the selenium cells was still a problem, but Baird was not discouraged. He obtained a better photo-electric cell and improved the way in which the signal was filtered and amplified. By 1923 he had built a unit that was able to transmit a blurry picture from one room of his laboratory to another. He built his apparatus out of an old hatbox using a pair of scissors, some darning needles, bicycle lamp lenses, a used tea chest, sealing wax, and glue.

Realizing how much work remained to be done, Baird attempted to get funding for his experiments. Investors, however, were less impressed with his results. London publisher J.W.B Odhams said, "We can see no future for a device which can only send shadows."[7] Despite the doubts of others,

Baird persevered. By 1926 he had improved his machine to the point where it was able to transmit a recognizable image of a face. He continued work on his "televisor," and by the early 1930s his machine was able to reproduce a thirty-line image. By this time Baird's work had captivated the public's imagination. About a thousand of his televisors were eventually produced and sold in England. Viewers were able to watch experimental broadcasts aired by Baird, and later, the British Broadcasting Company (BBC).

Charles Francis Jenkins

While Baird was working on his television system in England, Charles Francis Jenkins was following a similar path in the United States. Jenkins was a prolific American inventor who would eventually count more than four hundred U.S. patents to his credit. One was for a movie projector called the Phantoscope. He began concentrating his efforts on the transmission of moving pictures over wire in 1921.

Jenkins's approach involved using a series of prisms, as he had used in his film projector. His mechanical television system utilized a disk with forty-eight holes near the outer edge. A prism was mounted at each hole. The prism focused the light from the forty-eight lines of the image. By the spring of 1925, Jenkins, like Baird, was able to transmit blurred pictures with his "radiovision."

In 1928 the Federal Radio Commission (FRC), which had been created two years earlier to regulate radio transmissions in the United States, granted the first experimental television license to Jenkins Laboratories for station W3XK in Washington, D.C. Jenkins's broadcasts were basically images of animated silhouettes transmitted through the air.

Despite the successes of Baird and Jenkins, mechanical television systems based on the Nipkow disks had gone about as far as they could. The number of scans that could be produced in one second (a scan being one complete rotation of the disk) was limited by the speed at which the disk could revolve. It was impossible to make the disk spin fast enough to generate an image without noticeable flickering.

The Emmy Awards

Since 1949, the Academy of Television Arts and Sciences has been handing out its annual Emmy Awards to recognize outstanding achievements in the industry. The academy's founder, Syd Cassyd, originally proposed "Ike" for the name of the awards, that being the nickname given to the iconoscope tube. It was rejected because it was too closely associated with World War II hero—and future U.S. president—Dwight David "Ike" Eisenhower. The third academy president, Henry Lubcke, suggested "Immy" after the image orthicon tube that eventually succeeded the iconoscope. The name was eventually changed to the more feminine "Emmy" since the design of the statuette portrayed a woman holding an atom.

The very first Emmy was awarded in 1949 to twenty-year-old ventriloquist Shirley Dinsdale for Most Outstanding Television Personality. Five other awards were given out that year, including a special one to Louis McManus for designing the statuette, which was modeled by his wife.

In addition, the resolution or sharpness of the image produced was limited by the size and placement of the holes on the disk. Holes could not be made small enough—or placed close enough together—to produce a sharp picture. Given these limitations, it was hard to foresee a practical use for the technology. In order to improve the quality of the image on the screen, an entirely new technology was needed—an electrical method of image transmission based on the cathode ray tube.

Ferdinand Braun and the Cathode Ray Tube

German physicist Karl Ferdinand Braun made numerous contributions in the field of electricity. He shared the Nobel Prize in Physics with Marconi in 1909 for his work in wireless telegraphy. Braun's most important contribution to the development of television was the invention of what he called his "cathode ray indicator tube" in 1897.

Scientists knew that when voltage was applied between electrodes at opposite ends of a vacuum tube, a stream of

CATHODE RAY TUBE

Voltage is applied between electrodes at opposite ends of a vacuum tube, and a stream of electrons travels from the negatively charged electrode (the cathode) at one end of the tube to the positively charged electrode (the anode) at the other end. This beam of electrons is referred to as a cathode ray. The material phosphor emits light when struck by electrons.

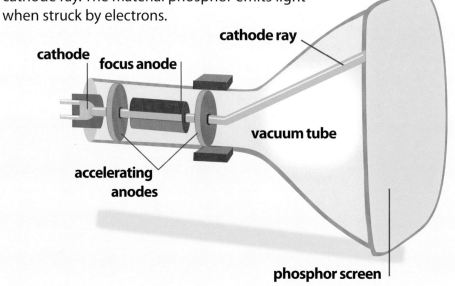

electrons traveled from the negatively charged electrode (the cathode) at one end of the tube to the positively charged electrode (the anode) at the other end. This beam of electrons was referred to as a cathode ray. Scientists also knew that certain materials, such as phosphor, emit light when struck by electrons.

Braun's creation consisted of a cathode ray tube with a phosphor-coated screen at one end. The screen glowed when the beam of electrons hit it. Braun improved on previous versions of the tube by alternating the voltage that was applied. Changing the voltage caused a change in the angle at which the ray was deflected onto the screen—the greater the voltage, the greater the angle of deflection. In this way the beam of electrons could be directed to trace a pattern on the screen. Braun's invention became an important laboratory research instrument. It would also be an important step in the development of future television systems.

The first man to envision using cathode ray tubes as a means of transmitting and receiving pictures was Scotsman A.A. Campbell Swinton, who did so as early as 1908. By 1920, however, he was still not convinced that such a system would ever actually work or that the technology would have any practical application. As he said in a speech before the Radio Society of Great Britain, the problem "is that it is probably scarcely worth anybody's while to pursue it. I think you would have to spend some years in hard work, and then would the result be worth anything financially?"[8]

It was left to a Russian engineer to take the next step.

Vladimir Zworykin and Electronic Television

Born in Murom, Russia, in 1889, Vladimir Zworykin studied at the St. Petersburg Institute of Technology under Boris Rosing. Rosing was doing experimental work on transmitting pictures by wire. His system employed an electronic cathode ray tube as a receiver and a mechanical Nipkow disk as a transmitter. He received a patent for his system in 1907.

Unfortunately the Russian Revolution interrupted Rosing's work, and he went into exile. Zworykin eventually made his way to the United States in 1919. He got a job at the Westinghouse Research Laboratory in Pittsburgh, Pennsylvania. While there, his work involved the development of radio tubes and photocells. He also continued to experiment with television.

In 1923 Zworykin applied for a patent for a television system that used a cathode ray tube, which he called an

BITS & BYTES

1927

Year of the first public demonstration of television in the United States

Shown is a model of the first picture receiver with cathode ray tube (left) and a Nipkow disk transmitter.

iconoscope, as a transmitter. An extensively revised version of the patent was not issued until 1938, however, since the equipment as originally described was never successfully demonstrated. Zworykin did display his system before a group of Westinghouse executives in the mid-1920s. It worked so poorly that they were not impressed. Zworykin later wrote, "I was terribly excited and proud, but after a few days I was informed, very politely, that my demonstration had been extremely interesting, but that it might be better if I were to spend my time on something 'a little more useful.'"[9]

David Sarnoff and RCA

Zworykin continued to work on his system on his own time. He eventually developed an improved cathode ray receiving tube that he called a kinescope. Zworykin's invention got the attention of David Sarnoff, vice president of the Radio Corporation of America (RCA), one of the largest manufacturers of radios in the country. Sarnoff had supported and financed the development of radio some years earlier. He was instrumental in the formation of the National Broadcasting Company (NBC) as a radio network in 1926.

By the early 1920s, Sarnoff had become convinced that advances in radio technology would eventually lead to the development of a workable television system. In a 1923 memo to the RCA board of directors, he wrote,

> I believe that television, which is the technical name for seeing instead of hearing by radio, will come to pass in due course. . . . Thus, it may well be expected that radio development will provide a situation whereby we shall be able actually to see as well as hear in New York,

Now known as one of the "fathers of television," Vladimir Zworykin's first attempts to demonstrate his television system in the mid-1920s were not very successful.

within an hour or so, the event taking place in London, Buenos Aires, or Tokyo."[10]

Sarnoff wanted RCA to take a leading role in bringing television technology to the public.

Sarnoff met Zworykin in January 1929. He asked how much it would cost to perfect his television system and how long it would take to develop it. Zworykin said it could be done in two years for a hundred thousand dollars. Sarnoff hired him as director of RCA's Electronic Research Laboratory in Camden, New Jersey. Years later, in relating this story to the *New York Times*, Sarnoff said, "RCA spent $50 million before we ever got a penny back from TV."[11]

Because of his contributions to the field, Zworykin is sometimes referred to as "the father of television." A young American inventor, however, is a challenger for the title.

Philo Farnsworth, Boy Visionary

Philo Taylor Farnsworth was born in a log cabin in Utah on August 19, 1906. When he was twelve years old, his family moved to a ranch in Rigby, Idaho. Farnsworth showed an interest in electronics at a very early age. When he was thirteen, he won a prize from *Science and Invention* magazine for a new type of automobile ignition switch that he developed.

It was the concept of television, however, that held the most fascination for Farnsworth. According to legend, one day while crisscrossing the fields of the family farm row by row with a harvesting machine, fourteen-year-old Farnsworth imagined light being transmitted by a beam of electrons in a similar line-by-line manner. He explained his idea to Justin Tolman, his chemistry teacher at Rigby High School. Instead of scanning an image mechanically through a Nipkow disk, his plan called for an electronic solution, using a cathode ray tube. Tolman recognized his student's brilliance and encouraged him to continue his experiments. Farnsworth's simple idea of line-by-line scanning was a basic principle that formed the foundation of modern television.

A Noteworthy Achievement

Farnsworth graduated from high school and entered Brigham Young University in 1923. There, he continued his research. With little money at his disposal, however, he could not afford to build the device that he envisioned. When his father died in early 1924, Farnsworth had to leave school to help provide for his family.

In 1926 Farnsworth married Elma "Pem" Gardner. The newlyweds moved to Los Angeles, California, where he found several investors willing to fund his experiments. By January of the next year, Farnsworth had finalized his plans. He applied for a patent for his electronic television camera tube, the "image dissector."

After redesigning several components of his system over the summer of 1927, Farnsworth was ready to try out his all-electronic television system on September 7. He painted a thick straight line on a glass slide. As he rotated it, the image was successfully transmitted to a receiver in the next room. Farnsworth recorded this momentous occasion in his journal with the simple phrase, "The received line picture was evident this time."[12] Despite his success, Farnsworth realized a great deal more work remained to be done before the general public could enjoy the benefits of his labors. He eventually demonstrated his system to members of the press the following year.

Farnsworth's accomplishments were reported by the *San Francisco Chronicle* in a 1928 article. According to the *Chronicle*, his invention produced "a queer looking little image in a bluish light now, one that frequently smudges and blurs, but the basic principle is achieved and perfection is now a matter of engineering."[13]

Sarnoff's Challenge

One of the people most interested in Farnsworth's work was David Sarnoff. Sarnoff had just offered Zworykin a position with RCA in 1930. He suggested Zworykin visit Farnsworth to see if he had developed anything that RCA could use

Philo Farnsworth demonstrates his all-electronic television receiver.

in its own quest to come up with an electronic television system. Unaware of Zworykin's true purpose, Farnsworth allowed him to visit and explore his lab for three days. The key component missing from Zworykin's system was a functioning electronic camera. He was impressed with Farnsworth's device and was overheard by witnesses to say, "This is a beautiful instrument. I wish that I might have invented it."[14]

The next spring Farnsworth reached an agreement with Philco, an up-and-coming radio manufacturer. Philco provided funding for his research, and in return, the company would profit from future royalties on his inventions. This venture was eventually reincorporated under the name Farnsworth Television.

Farnsworth had already obtained patents for several of his devices. The application Zworykin had filed for his iconoscope in 1923 was still being considered by the U.S. Patent Office, and a patent for it had not yet been issued. Sarnoff decided to visit Farnsworth's laboratories to decide for himself if the young inventor and his electronic television system were serious threats to his dream of controlling the television landscape. He was impressed enough by what he saw to offer Farnsworth one hundred thousand dollars for his patents and future services. Farnsworth declined the proposal since it would not allow him the freedom he had under his arrangement with Philco. Sarnoff returned to RCA, claiming little interest in Farnsworth's work. "There's nothing here we'll need,"[15] he announced.

BITS & BYTES
$100,000
Amount that RCA executive David Sarnoff offered Philo Farnsworth for his electronic television system patents

Farnsworth's work continued to progress and so did Zworykin's. In 1934 RCA unveiled a new electronic television system. A key component of the system was a new camera tube developed by Zworykin. RCA claimed this new iconoscope was basically the same device Zworykin tried to patent in 1923. That being the case, claimed RCA, then Farnsworth's image dissector came after the iconoscope and was an infringement on Zworykin's work. Farnsworth proceeded to challenge RCA's claim before the U.S. Patent Office.

Farnsworth vs. RCA

Sarnoff and RCA were not used to being challenged by smaller companies or to losing fights. He once reportedly said, "The RCA doesn't pay patent royalties, we collect them."[16] The giant corporation challenged Farnsworth's claim on three main points: the date the concept originated, when the patent application was filed, and when the device was operational.

To verify the first, Farnsworth brought in his old chemistry teacher, Justin Tolman. Tolman was able to duplicate Farnsworth's 1922 drawings of his system, supporting his claim as to when he came up with the idea. On the second point, Zworykin's 1923 filing date for his patent application could not be challenged. The third date was vital. Zworykin could not produce proof that his 1923 camera, as described in the patent application, actually worked. In April 1934 the patent examiner ruled in Farnsworth's favor. RCA appealed the decision, but the appeal was denied.

RCA eventually paid Farnsworth a licensing fee to use his patents in its television sets. It was the first time the giant corporation paid fees to use another person's technology. Sarnoff was ready to make his dream of bringing television to millions of Americans a reality.

CHAPTER **2**

The Networks Take Control

Having gained access to Farnsworth's patents, Sarnoff began his push to bring television to the American people. Sarnoff's plan consisted of three steps: to demonstrate the new technology in order to excite people about its possibilities for commerce, entertainment, and information; to mass produce sets and make them affordable for everyone; and, to make programming attractive to consumers. By doing this, RCA, through its broadcasting network, National Broadcasting Company (NBC), took a leading role in the television industry in the ensuing years. The Columbia Broadcasting System (CBS) and the American Broadcasting Company (ABC) followed NBC's lead, and the three networks guided television through its "golden age," the period during which television replaced radio as the primary source of entertainment for most Americans.

In order to ensure that television was operated in the best interests of the American people, the U.S. government took steps to oversee the growing industry. Its efforts were not always productive, however, and worries arose about the effects television programming had on the viewing public.

Government Regulation

Radio had been the American public's principal source of entertainment and information in the 1920s. It was controlled by NBC and CBS, which operated most of the hundreds of local stations across the country. Broadcast licenses were relatively easy to obtain. Stations, however, were limited to broadcasting over relatively few radio frequencies. This resulted in a state of disorder and confusion. Programs were often interrupted by others broadcasting over the same frequencies. Congress passed the Radio Act of 1927, which created the Federal Radio Commission (FRC) to regulate the airwaves in the United States. The commission was given the power to grant or deny licenses and to assign frequencies for each licensee.

RCA's Phantom Teleceiver

The RCA Pavilion was one of the most popular sites at the 1939 World's Fair. Designed by the architectural firm of Skidmore & Owings, it was shaped like a radio tube when viewed from the air. The purpose of the pavilion was to bring the wonders of television to the public.

Upon entering the lobby, visitors were greeted with the sight of a transparent version of the company's TRK-12 model television. The cabinet of the set was constructed out of clear, Lucite plastic. This enabled viewers to see the set's inner workings and assure them there was no trickery involved in how the images were produced. The television was soon christened the Phantom Teleceiver by the media.

The Phantom Teleceiver is currently housed in the MZTV Museum in Toronto, Canada.

On April 9 of that same year, Bell Laboratories gave the first American demonstration of television. The picture and voice of Secretary of Commerce Herbert Hoover were transmitted from Washington, D.C. to New York City. Hoover said, "Today we have, in a sense, the transmission of sight for the first time in the world's history. Human genius has now destroyed the impediment of distance in a new respect, and in a manner hitherto unknown."[17]

As the possibility of television becoming a new form of mass communication and entertainment grew, Congress passed the Communications Act of 1934. The act abolished the FRC and replaced it with the Federal Communications Commission (FCC). The FCC is responsible for regulating all communications originating in the United States, including radio, television, telephone, and telegraph. It has authority over the assignment of broadcast frequencies, rates and fees, standards, commercials, and broadcasting in the public interest. The FCC would play a major role in David Sarnoff's plans for the future of the television industry, a future he revealed to the world in 1939.

The 1939 World's Fair

The 1939 World's Fair in New York City gave Sarnoff the perfect opportunity to present the new technology to the public. The RCA pavilion at the fair featured a variety of television sets produced by the company. Several other companies, including Westinghouse Electric and General Electric, demonstrated their own models at their pavilions, also based on Farnsworth's technology.

The fair officially opened on April 30, 1939, with President Franklin D. Roosevelt's opening ceremonies speech. Members of the media eagerly anticipated the event. In the *New York Times* columnist Orrin Dunlap wrote,

> With all the exuberance of a boy with a new Kodak [camera], the radio men pick up their electric cameras today and go to the World's Fair to televise the opening spectacle and to telecast President Roosevelt as a "first" in this new category of broadcasting. And so by sunset tonight television will have come from around the corner in quest of its destiny: to find its role in the art of amusing Americans, and to fit in with the social life of the land.[18]

Roosevelt's remarks were followed up by an assortment of programs that were broadcast each day. Visitors to the fair were especially impressed with cameras set up at the RCA pavilion that enabled them to see themselves on TV. The public demonstration of television was a huge success.

Following the opening of the World's Fair, NBC began a regular schedule of television programming. From May through December 1939, the station broadcast from twenty to fifty-eight hours of shows per month, from Wednesday through Sunday of each week. Approximately one-third of the programming was devoted to news. Dramas accounted for 29 percent of programming hours and educational programming accounted for 17 percent. CBS started its own programming schedule soon after. Now Sarnoff had to get television sets into American homes.

BITS & BYTES

12 inches

Screen size of RCA's most popular television model, the TRK-12, in 1939

Baby Steps

Several manufacturers made sets available for sale at prices ranging from two to six hundred dollars. RCA's initial entry in the field was the TRK-12. Although it was the most expensive of the company's four models at six hundred dollars, it was the most popular. The picture tube was so large that it was mounted vertically in the cabinet, so the screen lay horizontal to the viewer. The set had a mirror in its lid that reflected the image from the 12-inch (30cm) screen.

These early sets appealed only to the wealthy. The cost of a television was out of the price range of the average worker,

Early television sets were placed in large cabinets, had small screens, and cost hundreds of dollars. At first only the wealthy could afford to buy them.

who was making three thousand dollars a year. Only about five thousand sets were sold by 1940, far below the number envisioned by Sarnoff and others. One observer that year wrote, "Television during the past year suffered as stormy a fate as ever beset a branch of the radio industry."[19]

Sarnoff, however, still maintained great hopes for the new technology. He declared,

The ultimate contribution of television will be its service toward unification of the life of the nation, and, at the same time, the greater development of the life of the individual. We who have labored in the creation of this promising new instrumentality are proud to have this opportunity to aid in the progress of mankind. It is our earnest hope that television will help to strengthen the United States as a nation of free people and high ideals."[20]

The United States' entry into World War II in 1941 interrupted Sarnoff's master plan. Television manufacture and programming basically stopped as the U.S. government converted many factories to produce materials needed by the military, and people's work and creativity all went toward the war effort. The production of cathode ray tubes, for example, was focused on radar and other high-tech uses.

Although the manufacture of televisions was temporarily banned, other developments in the industry continued to take place.

The War Years

In April 1941 the FCC approved standards for the television industry that would remain in place for more than half a century. The standards called for television sets to produce 525-line images at a frequency of thirty frames per second. By establishing a standard, it ensured that viewers would be able to watch each network.

Also significant was the restructuring of the radio networks. NBC had been operating two radio networks, called

Red and Blue. The government claimed this unfairly limited competition, and the courts agreed. In 1943 NBC was forced to sell the Blue network, which eventually became the American Broadcasting Company. These major radio programming networks were destined to become the networks that dominated television for more than forty years.

Despite the restrictions placed on the manufacture of televisions during the war years, prospects for the industry remained bright. FCC chairman James Lawrence Fly expressed this optimism in 1942, stating a belief that "during the postwar period television will be one of the first industries arising to serve as a cushion against unemployment and depression. . . . There is no reason now apparent why we should not aim at a 50,000,000-set television industry mirroring the present 50,000,000-set standard broadcast [radio] industry."[21]

Peter Goldmark's Contribution

Part of the reason for Fly's optimism was because of advances made in the development of color television. John Logie Baird had been working on color television as early as 1926. It was not until World War II, however, that major advances were made in the technology.

Peter Goldmark was an engineer with CBS. He was inspired to produce a color system after watching the 1939 hit movie, *Gone with the Wind*. Goldmark said, "I could hardly think of going back to the phosphor images of regular black-and-white television. All through the long, four-hour movie I was obsessed with the thought of applying color to television."[22]

Goldmark eventually developed what was called a "field-sequential" color system. It consisted of a standard black-and-white camera and television receiver. A rotating disk with red, green, and blue filters was mounted in front of the camera lens. An image was scanned by the camera. A second, similar disk inside the receiver was synchronized to rotate at the same speed as the first disk, producing three separate images—one red, one green, and one blue. The three images were displayed in rapid sequence. The human eye fused these images to produce one color picture.

Goldmark displayed his color system before representatives of the FCC in 1941. Although the representatives were impressed, they believed that more work remained to be done before the system could be made available to the general public. The control circuitry was extremely complex, and the power required by the system was also much greater.

RCA's David Sarnoff was also interested in Goldmark's work.

RCA, CBS, and Color Television

Sarnoff feared that if the FCC approved CBS's color system, it would cut into RCA's domination of the television market since RCA was still producing black-and-white televisions and broadcasting only in black and white. He argued that since Goldmark's system was based on the older, less-reliable, mechanical technology, it "would set back the cause of our technology by a generation."[23] He also noted that the system

Frank Stanton, president of CBS, shows his company's color television to a member of the Federal Communications Commission. CBS's color televisions did not work with shows made in black and white, but RCA improved on the model and color televisions quickly became popular purchases.

would not be compatible with the quarter-million black-and-white sets that had already been sold. Sarnoff's arguments were a contributing factor in the FCC's 1947 decision to again decline to adopt the CBS color system as the industry standard.

After seeing a public demonstration of Goldmark's system in 1949, however, the public began clamoring for adoption of a color standard. Television critic Harriet Van Horne said, "It's beautiful beyond words. It's impossible not to marvel at it. And not to feel disappointed when the show ends and the screen goes dark."[24] The FCC eventually adopted the CBS system in 1950. CBS began color broadcasts the next year with the airing of its first program, *Premiere*. The show was broadcast from 4:35 to 5:34 P.M. on June 25, 1951. The show featured CBS chairman of the board William Paley and CBS president Frank Stanton making statements. Also appearing were entertainment personalities Arthur Godfrey, Faye Emerson, Ed Sullivan, Sam Levenson, Robert Alda, Isabel Bigley, and Garry Moore. Two days later, CBS aired the first regularly scheduled color television series, *The World Is Yours!* The majority of its programming, however, continued to be in black and white.

CBS was not in the business of manufacturing television sets. Since its color technology was not compatible with the black-and-white sets already on the market, only about two dozen of the nearly 12 million TVs that had been sold up to that time were capable of receiving programs broadcast in color. In April 1951 CBS purchased its own television manufacturer—Hytron—but it was not able to compete with RCA. CBS eventually stopped its color transmissions in October 1951.

In the meantime RCA had been pushing to develop its own all-electronic color television system. Unlike CBS's color technology, RCA's technology did not make older sets obsolete. The older televisions would be able to show color broadcasts, but in black and white. RCA's efforts were successful, and in 1953 the FCC adopted RCA's system as the new color standard for the industry.

RCA began producing color sets the next year, but sales were not as successful as Sarnoff had hoped. The price of a

HOW COLOR TELEVISION WORKS

When a color TV needs to create a red dot, it fires the red beam at the red phosphor. Similarly for green and blue dots. To create a white dot, red, green and blue beams are fired simultaneously -- the three colors mix together to create white. To create a black dot, all three beams are turned off as they scan past the dot. All other colors on a TV screen are combinations of red, green and blue.

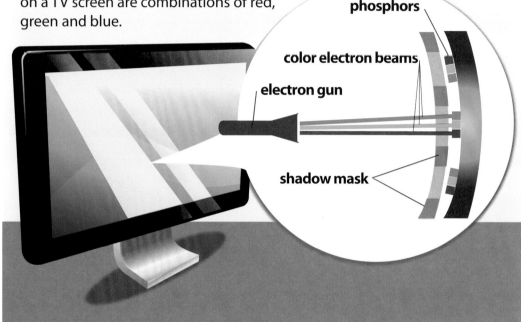

phosphors

color electron beams

electron gun

shadow mask

color set was much higher than that of a black-and-white model. In addition, there were few shows being broadcast in color. It was not until NBC aired *Walt Disney's Wonderful World of Color* in 1960 that color television began to catch on. By 1967 most shows were broadcast in color. Within another five years, as prices began to come down, color television sets could be found in about half the homes in the United States.

While NBC and CBS were busily engaged in the color war, many people were faced with a more immediate problem. They were unable to receive any television signals at all.

John Walson and Cable Television

Relatively few television stations were broadcasting in the late 1940s. For the most part, they were located in large metropolitan areas. Signals from these stations could not reach smaller cities and towns in mountainous or geographically remote areas of the country, so many people were denied access to the new technology.

In Mahanoy City, Pennsylvania, John Walson was the owner of a small appliance store. Few people in Mahanoy City were buying television sets. Although the town was just 90 miles (14km) from Philadelphia, it was situated in a valley where reception was very poor. The transmission of signals from Philadelphia was blocked by the surrounding mountains and could only be received along the ridges outside of town. Walson decided to do something about the problem.

In June 1948 Walson set up an antenna atop a utility pole on nearby New Boston Mountain. The antenna received the signals from Philadelphia and transmitted them to his store by means of coaxial cable. Coaxial cable, which basically is copper wire surrounded by insulation, is capable of transmitting various types of signals, including television and telephone signals.

This solved the problem. When local residents saw the results, they began buying televisions. Walson ran cables from the mountain antenna to his customers' homes. He eventually added amplification devices along the lines to improve the reception. Walson charged his customers one hundred dollars for installation and a monthly service charge of two dollars. Cable television, better known as Community Antenna Television (CATV), was born. Early cable providers offered viewers access to regular broadcast programming they would not otherwise have been able to receive. Special programming, such as the first-run movies and sporting events provided on cable today, was not available yet.

Cable television quickly spread across the country. By 1952 cable providers had approximately fourteen thousand subscribers nationwide. With more and more people having

Beavis and Butt-Head

Beavis and Butt-Head was an animated television series that aired on MTV from 1993 to 1997. The show featured a pair of obnoxious adolescents. Some critics praised the program as daring satire, while others panned it for its crude, offensive, juvenile humor.

The show made headlines in October 1993 when five-year-old Aaron Messner of Ohio set fire to his family's trailer, killing his two-year-old sister. The boy's mother said her son was inspired by the cartoon pair, who liked to burn things. In response, MTV agreed to air the program at a later time, when young children would be less likely to view it. MTV also agreed to delete references to fire in future shows.

In later months, the show was blamed as a negative influence in three more fires, a cat killing, and an incident in which a bowling ball was dropped from a highway overpass onto a car, killing an eight-month-old girl.

access to television programming, concerns arose about the appropriateness of what was being broadcast.

Viewing Violence on Television

The networks tried to attract as large an audience as possible. More viewers meant more advertising dollars, which translated into bigger profits. The most popular programs were the ones that gave viewers what they wanted to see. Many viewers enjoyed watching shows that were violent in nature or contained a violent component. In television's golden age, crime shows, Westerns, and action movies satisfied this desire for many people.

There were others, however, who objected to the amount of violence shown on television. In 1949 the Southern California Association for Better Radio and Television reported that over the course of one week of television shows over six Los Angeles stations—between the hours of 4 and 9 P.M.—members sat and watched ninety-one murders, seven holdups, three kidnappings, ten thefts, four burglaries, two cases of arson, two jailbreaks, two suicides, a homicidal explosion, one blackmail, and assorted cases of assault and battery and attempted murder. The following July television critic Jack Gould wrote in the *New York Times*,

> If radio and television aren't careful, somebody's going to call the cops. In their desperation to find inexpensive fillers for their summer schedules the two media have exceeded the bounds of reasonable interest in murder, mayhem and assorted felonies. Both the kilocycles and the channels are fairly dripping with crime and it is time that a halt was called."[25]

Gould had been motivated to voice his displeasure by the airing of a murder mystery immediately following a children's program on a Saturday morning.

Although the violence contained in these programs would be considered tame by modern standards, many people were upset. They believed programs depicting violence affected some viewers—particularly children—in a negative way. There was a call for government investigation into the matter.

Concerns about television programming finally got the attention of Congress. Representative E.C. Gathings of Arkansas introduced a resolution calling for congressional hearings on the topic. The resolution passed, and the first hearing took place in 1952.

Early Congressional Hearings

Gathings's resolution called for a subcommittee to "conduct a full and complete investigation and study to determine the extent to which the radio and television programs currently available to the people of the United States contain immoral and otherwise offensive matter, or place improper emphasis on crime, violence, and corruption."[26] The seven-member subcommittee, chaired by Oren Harris of Arkansas, held public hearings to discuss the problem. Industry representatives, government officials, and private citizens were called to testify. There was a general lack of organization to the hearings, however, and little was accomplished. Harris's position regarding the television industry was generally congenial. This may have been due to his recent purchase of a 25 percent interest in a Little Rock, Arkansas, television station. Although the

Oversight committee chairman Oren Harris held public hearings to discuss the quality of radio and television broadcasts in the mid-1950s. The hearings focused on issues such as television viewing and delinquency.

subcommittee's final report agreed that there was too much crime and violence on television, it called for self-regulation by the industry, with no government intervention.

Hearings held in 1954 and 1955 were more focused on the issues, particularly the relationship between television viewing and juvenile delinquency. Specific programs containing supposedly violent content were viewed and specific programming decisions questioned. The results, however, were basically the same. Representatives of the television industry argued that there was no evidence of a correlation between violence on television and criminal behavior among young viewers. They testified about the positive aspects of television and stressed that attempts to regulate programming were violations of their First Amendment rights. The committees ultimately called for additional research on the subject, continued attention to the issues on the part of the public, and promises by the industry to maintain self-regulation.

Talk, but Little Action

Although the television industry was criticized for poor programming, there was little call for government intervention. The FCC itself did not want the government to interfere in program content. It preferred to concern itself with the technological aspects of its responsibilities rather than content issues.

Becoming a Telecommunications Line Installer and Repairer

Job Description: Telecommunications line installers and repairers install and maintain the networks of lines and cables that provide individuals with access to phone, cable television, and the Internet.

Education: Most employers require a high school diploma or the equivalent. Vocational schools and community colleges offer courses in electronics and math that may prove helpful. Programs offering one-year certificates or more-advanced two-year associate degrees may be helpful but are rarely required by employers.

Qualifications: Knowledge of algebra and trigonometry are helpful, as are good reading and writing skills. Physical fitness, problem-solving skills, and the ability to work well with others are also prized. Employers often require formal apprenticeships or employer training programs that may combine on-the-job experience with classroom courses.

Additional Information: Entry-level workers may require three to five years of experience to reach the journeyman level and qualify to do most work without supervision. Additional years of experience are necessary to meet the requirements for first-line supervisor or trainer positions.

Salary Range: $24,700 to $68,200

Witnesses for the television industry continued to advocate self-regulation. They pointed to the National Association of Radio and Television Broadcasters' voluntary television code as an example of its dedication to quality programming. The group expressed its philosophy in the opening paragraph of the code, which read,

> Television is seen and heard in every type of American home. These homes include children and adults of all ages, embrace all races and all varieties of religious faith, and reach those of every educational background. It is the responsibility of television to bear constantly in mind that the audience is primarily a home audience, and consequently that television's relationship to the viewers is that between guest and host.[27]

The pattern of government concern about television programming, industry promises to improve self-regulation, and government reluctance to become more involved continued over the years. Despite numerous other congressional hearing on television violence, the guidelines established in the early 1950s remained in place. The public was assured that both Congress and the television industry were concerned with the effect of television on children, but no further significant action was taken by either side.

Violence in programming was not the only issue that concerned people. Some worried that increased viewing was contributing to a sedentary lifestyle. Since television involved watching and listening, audiences sat watching the TV, whereas they could combine other activities with their radio listening. The only time a person had to get up was to turn the set on and off and to switch channels. When Zenith introduced a wireless remote control in the mid-1950s, even that became easier to do.

The Remote Control

Although the first television remote control was not developed until 1950, the idea had been around for a long time. In 1898 Nikola Tesla described one in his patent for a "Method of And Apparatus For Controlling Mechanism of Moving Vessels or Vehicles." He gave a public demonstration of a radio-controlled boat at Madison Square Garden in New York that same year. Several radio manufacturers offered remote controls in the late 1930s. The first wireless remote was the Philco Mystery Control for radio, produced in 1939. The technology was used extensively by the military in World War II. Following the end of the war, remotes began being used for nonmilitary purposes, such as with garage door openers.

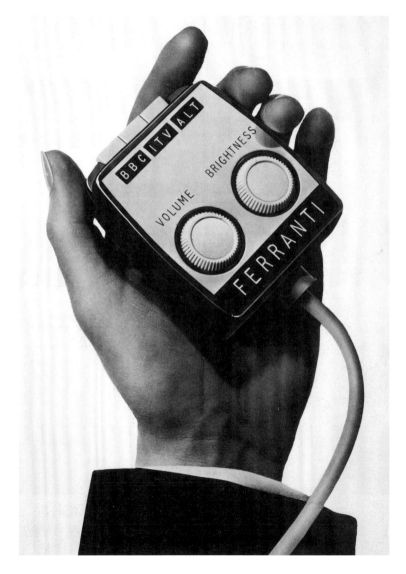

The first television remote control was developed in 1950. It was connected to the television by a cord, which people complained about tripping over.

By 1950 the Zenith Electronics Corporation (at the time called Zenith Radio Corporation) had entered the field of television. That year, it introduced Lazy Bones, the first television remote control. Lazy Bones was able to turn a TV set on and off and to change channels. It did so by connecting to an electric motor on the set with a cable. The motor turned the tuner either clockwise or counterclockwise to get different stations.

Although the remote worked, users complained about tripping over the bulky cable. That problem was solved five years later with the introduction of the first wireless television remote. The Flash-Matic was invented by Zenith engineer Eugene Polley. It operated by aiming a type of flashlight at photocells located in each corner of the television cabinet surrounding the screen. Unfortunately the photocells could not differentiate between various sources of light. If the TV was placed where light from a window shone directly on it, the tuner might start rotating and change stations.

Robert Adler Steps In

Zenith engineers considered radio and sound signals as replacements for the photocell technology, but both were eventually rejected. Robert Adler finally suggested using ultrasonics. Ultrasonics are high-frequency sounds outside the human range of hearing. Adler's first transmitter design was built around a series of aluminum rods that emitted high-frequency sounds when struck at one end. Called the Zenith Space Command, the device went on the market in 1956. It was the first practical wireless television remote control.

The original Space Command was expensive. It raised the cost of a television by approximately 30 percent since the receiver in the set required an additional six vacuum tubes in order to operate. In spite of its cost, the remote became popular with consumers and other manufacturers soon followed Zenith's lead. As Adler's patent application states, "It is highly desirable to provide a system to regulate the receiver operation without requiring the observer to leave the normal viewing position."[28]

By the 1960s transistors began replacing vacuum tubes. Transistors were smaller, faster, generated less heat, and were less costly to produce. The cost of the remote dropped, and it was made smaller. Adler's ultrasonic technology remained the standard for remote controls until the 1980s. At that point, it was replaced by infrared (IR) technology. In these new devices, a signal is sent to the set by a low-frequency light beam that cannot be seen by the human eye.

Although remotes made viewing easier, they did nothing to affect what was being viewed. More and more people began criticizing television programming.

Tiny transistors (center) were smaller and faster than the larger vacuum tubes they replaced. Transistors were incorporated into remote controls, which allowed those items to also be made smaller.

Newton Minow and the "Vast Wasteland"

One of the loudest critics was FCC chairman Newton Minow. Speaking before the National Association of Broadcasters shortly after his appointment as FCC chairman in 1961,

Minow issued one of the more scathing attacks on the state of television. He challenged his audience to

> sit down in front of your television set when your station goes on the air and stay there, for a day, without a book, without a magazine, without a newspaper, without a profit and loss sheet or a rating book to distract you. Keep your eyes glued to that set until the station signs off. I can assure you that what you will observe is a vast wasteland."[29]

Minow's criticism of commercial television sparked a debate over the future of the medium. Never before had an FCC chairman criticized the industry to such a degree. "Vast wasteland" became a catchphrase signifying all that was wrong with programming content. Despite Minow's call for reform, however, there was little he could do to affect what was broadcast without the support of Congress.

CHAPTER 3

A Variety of Choices

In the early years of television, the number of people who could receive signals was limited to those who lived in relative close proximity to a broadcasting station. New technology brought television to all parts of the country. With the advent of cable satellite service, the invention of the videocassette recorder, and the popularity of video games, people had even more reasons to spend their time sitting in front of the set.

Transmitting Signals

The first television stations transmitted signals through the air from broadcast towers to antennas that were set up on rooftops to receive them. Unfortunately, this severely limited the number of people who could receive signals. The signal got weaker as the distance from the broadcasting station increased. In addition, mountains and other large objects interfered with transmission in some remote areas.

For many people, these problems were solved by cable television, which was first introduced in the late 1940s. After an antenna picked up the signal, it was amplified and transmitted to individual homes through coaxial cables laid in the ground.

By the early 1950s the owners of cable systems began using microwaves to receive signals from distant cities. This increased the number of stations that could be received,

giving viewers a wider variety of program choices. Cable signals also provided sharper, clearer pictures that further attracted subscribers. Together, these two factors made cable an attractive option for more and more people. By the early 1960s about 850,000 people had access to cable television.

The Birth of HBO

The event that arguably had the biggest effect on the popularity of cable occurred in November 1972, when pay television was launched. That month, John Walson's company began offering Home Box Office (HBO) to its customers in Wilkes-Barre, Pennsylvania.

Charles Dolan conceived the idea for HBO in 1971. Dolan was the owner of Sterling Communication, a firm that provided cable service in New York City. Dolan's idea was for a subscription television service that would attract customers by offering first-run movies and sporting events. He originally named this service the Green Channel. The Green Channel was subsidized by Time Inc. It was renamed Home Box Office and debuted on November 8, 1972. At the time the service began, HBO had 365 subscribers in Wilkes-Barre. Its first offerings were *Sometimes a Great Notion*, a movie starring Paul Newman, and a National Hockey League game between the New York Rangers and the Vancouver Canucks from Madison Square Garden in New York.

Like many new ventures, HBO lost money at first. Dolan was fired and lawyer Gerald Levin replaced him as president. The channel continued to struggle until 1975 when it made a move that would have a major effect on the cable industry. That year, Levin signed a six-year contract that allowed HBO to distribute its programming by means of communications satellite.

BITS & BYTES

170 pounds

Weight of the Telstar 1 communications satellite

Telstar

Telstar 1 was the first experimental communications satellite to transmit both telephone and television signals. Owned by AT&T (originally American Telephone & Telegraph Company), it was built by a team of engineers at Bell Telephone Laboratories and launched aboard a Delta rocket from Cape Canaveral, Florida, on July 10, 1962. The next day it relayed its first picture, the U.S. flag outside the company's ground station in Andover, Maine. Thirteen days later, Telstar transmitted the first live transatlantic television signals from space. A press conference of President John F. Kennedy was relayed from Washington, D.C., across the Atlantic Ocean, to Pleumeur-Bodou, France. That night, it also transmitted its first telephone call.

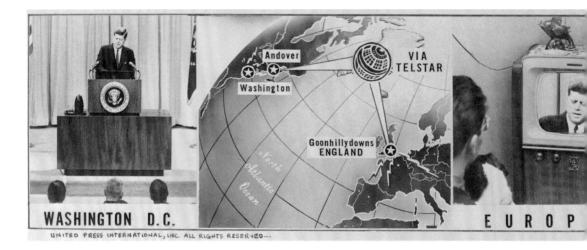

WASHINGTON D.C.

EUROP

The Telstar satellite allowed for long-range communications. As the illustration shows, with the development of Telstar a press conference by U.S. president John F. Kennedy could now be transmitted and received in Europe.

In simple terms, broadcast signals are transmitted from the ground station to the satellite. They are bounced off the satellite and can be picked up by any satellite receiver dish that has a view of it. Because of its orbit, Telstar was only available to transmit signals for a limited period of time each day.

In time several satellites were placed in geosynchronous orbits. This means the satellites have the same rotational velocity as the earth, and an antenna on the ground can maintain a continual link with a satellite. Once satellites became part of national telecommunications, the Federal Communications Commission (FCC) decided it wanted to regulate cable.

The FCC and Cable

When cable television first emerged in 1948, the FCC avoided interfering with it. The Communications Act of 1934 only charged it with regulating communications sent over the airwaves. In 1956 the FCC decided it had no jurisdiction over cable since signals were sent through wires rather than through the air.

The networks were concerned, however, because cable providers were transmitting network signals to subscribers and charging a fee for the service. By 1962 the FCC had changed its stance, deciding cable was within its jurisdiction

U.S. HOUSEHOLDS WITH CABLE TELEVISION, 1975-2009

The number of households with cable television increased every year from 1975 to 2001.
The number then began decreasing as households moved to satellite and internet television.

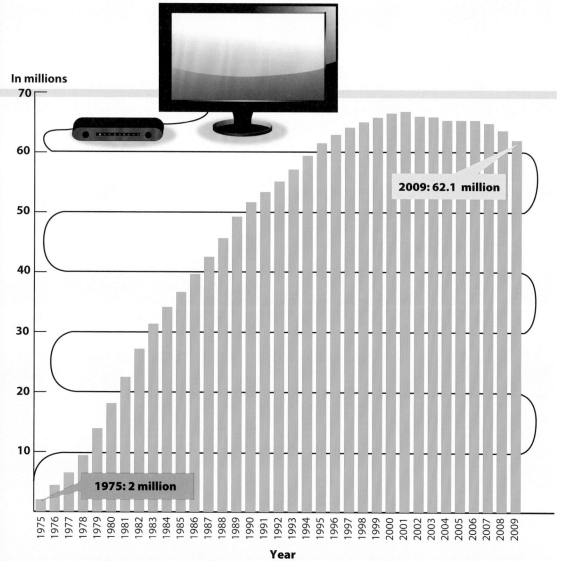

In millions

2009: 62.1 million

1975: 2 million

Year

Taken from: National Cable & Telecommunications Association, "Basic Video Customers 1975—2009,"
http://www.ncta.com/Stats/BasicCableSubscribers.aspx.

because it involved broadcast television. Over the next few years, the FCC issued regulations that limited the growth of cable. These included limiting service to areas where network broadcast television could not be received and forbidding the broadcast of recent sporting events and new movies.

These rulings stirred up a public backlash. Cable subscribers were upset that they were not allowed access to new stations that appeared on the market. The FCC was forced to respond. In 1972 it issued a Cable Television Report and Order that eased some of the restrictions. In particular, the report eased the restrictions on importing distant signals into the top one hundred broadcast markets. It still limited the number of signals a given system could carry, however. This gave cable operators a wider choice in the types of signals they could offer to subscribers.

Television and Health

As television has offered more and more channels to watch, viewers are spending more and more time in front of their television sets. Evidence has begun to accumulate suggesting that the increased amount of time watching television is having a negative effect on viewer health. Of all possible leisure-time activities, watching television is arguably the unhealthiest.

As individuals become more and more inactive, obesity and other health problems increase. In the United States, the percentage of children and adolescents who are overweight has more than tripled since 1970. Some experts say television viewing is a major contributor to this disturbing trend, particularly among children. William H. Dietz, obesity expert at Tufts University School of Medicine, says, "The easiest way to reduce inactivity is to turn off the TV set. Almost anything else uses more energy than watching TV."

Quoted in Barbara Brock. "Life Without TV: Filling Those Four Hours with More Satisfying Leisure." *Parks & Recreation*, November 2002, http://findarticles.com/p/articles/mi_m1145/is_11_37/ai_95107110.

Cable Satellite Service

In 1975 the FCC issued a ruling permitting satellites to be used to broadcast television signals. That September HBO broadcast the heavyweight championship fight between Muhammad Ali and Joe Frazier live from Manila in the Philippines, using signals relayed from the Satcom I satellite. The bout, billed as the "Thrilla in Manila," was won by Ali in fourteen rounds. It was an instant classic, and a huge success for HBO. The company proceeded to take the FCC to court, claiming it had no right to limit programming options. HBO won and the FCC restrictions were eventually overturned.

In 1976 the number of HBO subscribers jumped from 15,000 to nearly 290,000. By the end of 1977 HBO was finally showing a profit, with approximately 600,000 customers. Other cable channels followed HBO's lead in using satellite delivery of their services. These included the Turner Broadcasting System (TBS), Showtime, the Entertainment and Sports Programming Network (ESPN), and Music Television (MTV).

The 1975 boxing match between Muhammad Ali and Joe Frazier was broadcast live via satellite from the Philippines. The FCC only started to allow satellites to broadcast television signals in 1975.

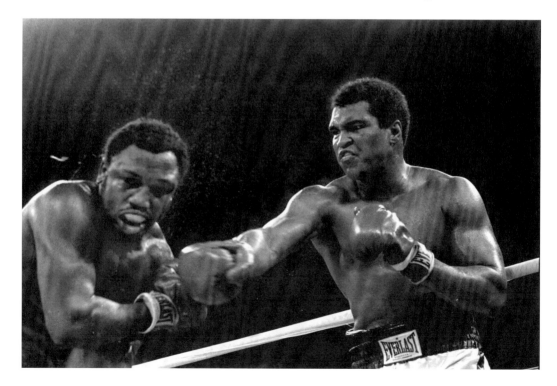

Cable was no longer a service that merely brought network television to areas of the country that could not receive transmissions directly through the air. It had become a fee-based service that brought customers a wide range of channels and improved reception. HBO president Gerald Levin was hailed by *Channels* magazine as "the man who started the revolution."[30]

Cable television gave viewers access to more channels than ever before. No longer were viewers limited to programming provided by the networks. Some media leaders questioned the need for such variety. Sumner Redstone, president and CEO of media giant Viacom, said, "I am very skeptical of this talk of 500 channels. I just don't know what's going to play on them."[31]

Reflecting a Changing Society and Culture

The increase in the number of channels was particularly significant for minority viewers. Throughout the 1950s and 1960s, television basically ignored minority viewers. Programmers assumed whites made up the bulk of the viewing audience and directed their efforts toward this majority. The few minority figures that did find their way onto the screen were generally presented as stereotypes.

One program that depicted African Americans in this way was CBS's *Amos 'n' Andy*, which was broadcast from 1951 through 1953. Although the show was popular with viewers, it was also targeted as being racist. In a 1989 article in the *New York Times* author and professor Henry Louis Gates Jr. wrote, "The performance of those great black actors . . . transformed racist stereotypes into authentic black humor. The dilemma for 'Amos 'n' Andy,' however, was that these were the only images of blacks that Americans could see on TV. The political consequences for the early civil rights movement were thought to be threatening."[32] The National Association for the Advancement of Colored People (NAACP) brought pressure on the network, and the show was taken off the air in 1953.

The popular CBS show Amos 'n' Andy *depicted African American characters in a way critics termed racist. At the time these were the only depictions of blacks on American TV. The show was taken off the air in 1953 after pressure from the NAACP.*

The civil rights movement of the 1960s and 1970s helped bring the issue of minorities in television to the forefront by raising the public's awareness of the issue. Slowly but surely more television programs began to feature minority actors in leading roles. Black actor and comedian Bill Cosby costarred in the 1965 hit series, *I Spy*, eventually garnering three Emmy Awards for his work. The show was the first to feature an African American actor in a lead role. Three years later the sitcom *Julia*, starring Diahann Carroll, made its debut. Carroll was the first black woman to star in a prime-time series.

Another breakthrough occurred in 1974 when comedian Freddie Prinze became the first Hispanic to star in a show. His show, *Chico and the Man*, aired on NBC until 1978.

African Americans began to appear more often on prime-time shows, with programs like *The Flip Wilson Show* (1970–74), *Good Times* (1974–79), *The Jeffersons* (1975–85), and *The Cosby Show* (1984–92), all drawing large audiences. The eight-part miniseries *Roots* was a huge hit in 1977. It traced the lives of members of an African American family through four generations.

The era of cable television opened the door to more programming for minorities than ever before. Broadcasters began directing their efforts toward African Americans, Hispanics, Asians, women, gays, and other minorities. Today there are entire cable networks devoted to minority broadcasting. These include Black Entertainment Television (BET), Telemundo (programming in Spanish), Women's Entertainment (WE tv), and others.

The Videocassette Recorder

It would not be long before another technological breakthrough gave viewers another choice: when to watch programs that they wanted to see. This became possible with the invention of the home videocassette recorder (VCR).

Up through the mid-1950s, all television programs were broadcast live. Networks recorded programs on film, but viewers were at the mercy of network programmers. They could only watch programs when they were broadcast. In 1950 CBS's chief engineer Howard Chinn had suggested an option that would allow for editing, replays, and more overall flexibility. "Why not store the video signal on magnetic tape?" asked Chinn. "Such a scheme would use up a lot of tape, but it might well be worth it."[33]

Such recording was already being done with audio. Video, however, presented a greater problem since much more data had to be recorded. A group of engineers at Ampex Corporation in California came up with an answer. The group, led by Charles Ginsburg, developed the first practical reel-to-reel videotape recorder (VTR) in 1956. Since the Ampex

VRX-1000 (later renamed the Mark IV) cost fifty thousand dollars, only networks and larger stations could afford the equipment. CBS became the first network to employ the new technology, doing so that same year. The first program to be broadcast via videotape was *Douglas Edward and the News* on November 30.

Nine years later, Sony unveiled the CV-2000. At approximately one thousand dollars, it was a less expensive, reel-to-reel machine, designed specifically for home use. Not many were sold, however, since the unit was complicated to operate and did not produce quality pictures. Ampex and RCA followed with machines of their own, but the public was reluctant to buy a VTR that used the reel-to-reel technology. Such VTRs required that a tape be threaded by hand through rollers, across tape heads, and onto a take-up reel in the machine. This made the tape extremely susceptible to damage and contamination.

Sony began concentrating its efforts on developing a cassette format. The result was the U-Matic system, introduced in 1971. The U-Matic was the first videocassette recorder (VCR) meant for commercial use. It became popular with schools and businesses, but its thirteen-hundred-dollar price tag kept it out of the range of most consumers.

Home Videocassette Recorders

The Dutch electronics firm Philips took the next step. Philips released its 1500 model in England in 1972. It was the first videocassette recorder marketed specifically for home use. The machine used cassettes that could hold up to sixty minutes of footage. It also came with a clock that allowed the user to record a program up to twenty-four hours in advance. Unfortunately, because of its relatively high price, it was used mostly by businesses and in schools. It was not a big seller in the home market.

VCR design continued to improve. Sony came out with the Betamax system (also called Betacord or simply Beta)

Sony issued the Betamax videocassette recorder system in 1975. It allowed users to record a TV show and watch it later.

in November 1975. It was more technically advanced and more reliable than the Philips machines. The next year, the Video Home System (VHS) format appeared on the market as Betamax's main competition. VHS machines boasted a longer recording time (two hours compared to one) than Betamax units. Although Betamax was generally considered to have better picture quality, VHS gained in popularity. By 1980 VHS machines accounted for approximately 70 percent of the VCR market.

Sony Takes on Universal

Soon after Sony introduced the Betamax, questions arose as to the legality of taping television programs. Hollywood studios, led by Universal and Disney, filed a lawsuit claiming that doing so was a violation of copyright law. One worry was that if programs were taped for later viewing, users were more likely to skip through the commercials. This could potentially reduce the revenue for the advertisers who were ultimately paying for the program.

Sony Corp. of America v. Universal City Studios, Inc. dragged on through the courts for several years. The district court ruled against Universal and Disney, but the Ninth Circuit Court of Appeals reversed the decision. Finally in 1984—eight years after the suit was originally filed—the U.S. Supreme Court reversed the ruling of the Ninth Circuit Court. It ruled that taping shows for home viewing was legal. Such taping was a fair use of the copyrighted material and thus did not violate the Copyright Act. The fair-use doctrine allows reproduction of copyrighted works in certain cases. Teachers, for example, can reproduce portions of a copyrighted book for teaching purposes without obtaining permission from the author.

The ruling gave a boost to an already growing industry. Nearly 8 million VCRs were sold that year, along with approximately 160 million blank cassettes purchased for recording

Closed-Captioning

Closed-captioning displays on the television screen the words being spoken in a television program, so viewers can read the dialog. This is helpful for hearing-impaired viewers, those trying to learn English, and viewers in a noisy environment, such as a bar or airport terminal. "Closed" refers to the fact that the text is not visible to everyone, only those who choose to activate it.

The Television Decoder Circuitry Act of 1993 required all analog sets with screens 13 inches (33cm) or larger to contain decoding circuitry. The captions are hidden in the part of the television signal called the vertical blanking interval.

A human operator is responsible for making transcriptions of live programs by using a stenomask type of machine. The stenomask is a mouth mask with a built-in microphone. The speech-to-text reporter speaks into the microphone, and the output is instantly translated into text by a computer. The mask allows the person to speak without disturbing other people.

programs. The entertainment industry also benefited, through the rental and sale of prerecorded movies.

Video Stores

The popularity of the VCR gave rise to the concept of video rentals. Los Angeles businessman George Atkinson was the owner of a company that rented movies and projectors to groups for parties. In 1977 he opened the Video Station on Wilshire Boulevard. He rented videos for ten dollars a day, charging fifty dollars for an annual membership and a hundred dollars for a lifetime membership. The store was a success and Atkinson soon expanded to other cities. By 1984 the Video Station had five hundred stores. Hollywood studios began offering more and more of their films for sale and rental, and prices dropped, as did those for VCRs.

Video Games

In addition to movies, video stores also began renting and selling video games. The first video games date back to the 1950s. These games were designed to be played on mainframe computers housed at universities like the Massachusetts Institute of Technology (MIT). It was not until 1966 that work began on the first home console system. The idea came to New Hampshire engineer Ralph Baer, who jotted down some notes while watching television one evening. Baer says, "When I got back to my office in New Hampshire on September 1, 1966, I transcribed those notes into a 4-page paper, a Disclosure Document which described the idea of playing television games on a home TV set."[34]

By 1968 the first working demonstration model of Baer's system, called the Brown Box, was ready. Magnavox became the first licensee. The company released its version, called the Magnavox Odyssey system, in 1972. The system was a huge success, with nearly a hundred thousand being sold that first year. It marked the beginning of the home TV game market.

The industry exploded by mid-decade with the development of integrated circuits. The cost of production went down, and quality of performance went up. It was not long

before companies like Atari, Nintendo, and Sony came out with their own systems.

The most recent generation of games was inspired by the introduction of the Nintendo Wii in 2006. Players interact with the Wii by using motion-based control devices, such as the Wii remote and Nintendo's Balance Board. In 2010 the XBox 360 Kinect was introduced. With this game system, the user interacts with the TV without a controller and, in effect, becomes the controller. This suggests that similar devices or methods of interaction might be employed by future generations of televisions.

The first video games dated to the 1950s and quickly changed with technology. In the 1980s, companies like Atari, Nintendo, and Sony came out with their own highly popular video game systems.

CHAPTER 4

Improving the Product

There were relatively few major advances in television technology from the 1940s through the 1990s. The introduction of color TV in the 1950s was probably the most significant. Since the 1990s, however, several improvements have been made to enhance the viewing experience, and to increase the options available to viewers.

Interactive Television

Interactive television means different things to different people, with varying degrees of interactivity. In its simplest form, interactive television began in the 1950s. One of the earliest examples was the show *Winky Dink and You*. Viewers were able to buy a clear cellophane sheet that was placed on the television screen. At various points in the program, they were asked to help the lead cartoon character by drawing different items on the "magic screen" with their "magic crayons." This included things such as a bridge to help Winky Dink cross a river.

QUBE

The QUBE system developed by Warner Communications was the world's first commercial interactive television service. It became available in Columbus, Ohio, in late 1977. The thirty channels offered by QUBE included ten for

Interactive TV, in which the viewer can participate in and influence events on the television, was explored in the late 1970s, but failed to become popular enough to be sustained until the mid-1990s.

broadcast television, ten for pay-per-view options, and ten for interactive fare. QUBE's chief engineer Paul Dempsey recalls, "QUBE was the first to offer first-run movies on a pay-per-view basis, other than a few hotels."[35]

The idea for QUBE came to Warner president Steve Ross from a closed-circuit television system developed by Pioneer Electronics for the Otani Hotel in Japan. Ross became fascinated with the idea of delivering Warner's movies directly to home cable subscribers.

QUBE's interactive channel included talk shows where the viewing audience responded to questions, as in an opinion poll. They did so by pressing one of a series of buttons on the QUBE remote. The system also included interactive games and auctions where viewers interacted by pressing buttons on the QUBE remote control. Other channels let younger viewers register for community education programs or choose musical footage from various outlets. Included among the community channels was Pinwheel, which would eventually be renamed Nickelodeon in 1981. Other selections included a weather channel and a learning channel.

QUBE spread to several other cities, but the cost of operating the only two-way cable system in the country became prohibitive. Eventually American Express became an investor but that was not enough to save the company. John Carey of Columbia University explains, "The service cost a fortune to deliver. The QUBE set-top box alone cost $200 at a time when cable converters cost $40. . . . Further, there were reliability problems with the equipment, especially in the data transmission upstream from homes to the cable headend."[36] QUBE eventually went out of business in 1994.

Although many people considered QUBE a failure, not everyone shared that view. Carey says,

> Half the households in Columbus paid to get QUBE usage and they created a lot of innovative programming, inventing the pay-per-view business. Despite the high subscription rates, however, actual usage was generally low, with exceptions. . . . QUBE demonstrated that pay-per-view was viable, if the cost of promoting and processing pay-per-view orders could be reduced."[37]

Internet Television

Another level of interactivity became possible in 1994 with the emergence of Internet television, a television service that is distributed over the Internet. Viewers can watch videos that are "streamed" directly to their computer. This means a viewer does not have to wait for a video to be downloaded first before it can be played. A streaming video plays instantly, without any pause or interruption. Programs can also be downloaded to a user's hard drive for viewing at a later time. When viewing over the Internet, a person is not limited to watching a program when it is broadcast. Even shows that have been off the air for years can be found, usually with fewer commercials than on broadcast television.

The first television show broadcast over the Internet was *ABC's World News Now* in 1994. Since then, many websites have made video broadcasts available, including network sites. Other sites, such as Hulu, provide short clips from shows, complete episodes, entire seasons, and even exclusive "webisodes" available only over the Internet.

The Analog to Digital Transition

Many of the changes involving interactive television—and those envisioned for the future—are made possible through the emergence of digital television (DTV). Until 2009, all television transmissions were made by means of analog signals. Such electromagnetic signals are in the form of energy composed of waves. These waves are subject to interference by other waves, which can disrupt, or change, the signal.

By contrast, digital signals are electronic signals that send data encoded as long strings of zeroes and ones, known as binary code. These strings of code can be understood by a variety of digital devices, such as televisions, computers, cell

Streaming video on Internet TV allows viewers to watch programs as they are happening through their computer instead of through their television set. Many shows now offer online broadcasts.

Becoming a Television Repairperson

Job Description: A television repairperson's job includes repairing TVs and VCRs, installing audio equipment, and repairing home theater systems.

Education: Most employers require a high school diploma or the equivalent. Some vocational schools and community colleges offer 2-year courses in television repair that may prove helpful in obtaining a job. Others offer associate degrees in electronics technology, which combine fundamentals, theory and hands-on training.

Qualifications: Applicants should have a knowledge of electronics, related hands-on experience, good customer service skills, and good problem-solving skills.

Additional Information: A new entrant in the field may work as an apprentice to gain experience. Although certification is not required for entry-level positions, it increases the chances of finding employment. Certification is offered by various organizations, such as the Electronics Technicians Association (ETA).

Salary Range: $26,100 to $40,900

phones, and MP3 players. The digital signals are much less susceptible to interference or change than analog signals. They can also be compressed so that more information can be transmitted in less space. Because of these advantages, the Federal Communications Commission (FCC) mandated that all television broadcasters make the transition from analog to digital signals. This transition went into effect on June 12, 2009. One of the advantages of digital signals is that they make high-definition television (HDTV) possible. This necessitated a revamping of the National Television System Committee (NTSC) standards for television.

The 1941 Standards

The guidelines for television transmission in the United States approved by the FCC in 1941 remained in place for several decades. These guidelines, as suggested by the National Television System Committee (NTSC), the group established by the FCC to resolve conflicts concerning television transmission standards, included 525 lines per picture, 30 frames per second, a maximum resolution of 720 by 486 pixels, and an aspect ratio of 4:3. The standards had been established as a compromise between the system used by RCA sets and the higher-resolution system proposed by Philco Television.

The number of pixels that can fit on the screen determines the resolution, or sharpness, of the picture. The word *pixel* stands for "picture element." A pixel is the smallest piece of an image. It is a tiny rectangular dot comprised of three smaller color dots, one red, one blue, and one green. Because they are so close together on the screen, these three dots appear to blend together into a single color. NTSC sets can display a picture 720 pixels wide by 486 pixels high, so one complete image can consist of a total of 349,920 pixels.

The aspect ratio is the ratio of the width of the screen compared to the height. A ratio of 4:3, for example, means that a screen 20 inches (51cm) wide will be 15 inches

The number of pixels that fit on a television screen determine its resolution. Pixels are the small, rectangular dots comprised of red, blue, and green that blend together to create the pictures generated on a TV screen.

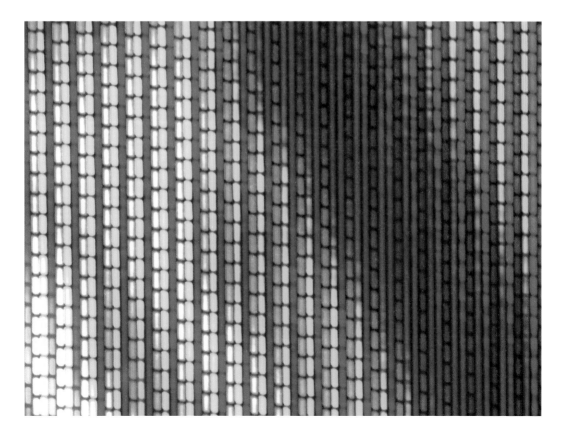

(38cm) high. The 4:3 ratio dates back to 1889. It was developed by W.K.L. Dickson, who was working on a motion-picture camera for Thomas Edison Laboratories in New Jersey. Dickson made the film for the camera 1-inch (2.5cm) wide and 3/4-inch (1.9cm) high. This became the standard for the motion-picture industry and was adopted as the standard for television by the FCC.

Since people have two eyes, their field of vision is more rectangular than square. The movie industry tried to take advantage of this fact in the 1950s by experimenting with films that used a widescreen format, such as *Cinerama*. An aspect ratio of 16:9—fit to the peripheral vision of the human eyes—produced very positive results. It is the most common aspect ratio currently used for movie screens. Television, however, continued to stick with the 4:3 ratio until the onset of high-definition TV.

Japan in the Forefront

The Japanese developed the first high-definition television system for consumer use. The Japan Broadcasting Corporation (Nippon Hoso Kyokai) began work on developing the next generation of television in the 1960s. The result was a high-definition television that provided a much sharper picture as well as improved sound. With 1,125 lines of resolution, a rate of 60 frames per second, and an aspect ratio of 16:9, the system became known as Hi-Vision, or more commonly MUSE, after the form of compression it used. MUSE received positive reviews when it was first demonstrated in the United States in 1981. The only drawback was that the system required 20 megahertz of bandwidth, over three times the bandwidth allotted to broadcasters under the existing NTSC system. Because of this, the FCC refused to authorize MUSE and systems similar to it. The FCC insisted that broadcasters be limited to the 6 megahertz of space allowed by the 1941 standards.

By this time Japan had taken the clear lead in television production. Only one U.S. company still manufactured sets.

American firms were concentrating on developing cable and satellite television systems that could deliver multiple channels. In 1987 the FCC established the Advisory Committee on Advanced Television Service (ACATS). The committee was charged with reviewing the available digital technology and recommending an advanced television service (ATS) to the FCC.

General Instrument and the Grand Alliance

It did not take the ACATS long to determine that digital technology was superior to analog. The seven companies involved in developing ATS—AT&T, General Instrument,

High definition television allows for more pixels on the screen and thus a clearer, more detailed picture.

MIT, Philips, Sarnoff, Thomson, and Zenith—decided to pool their resources in 1993 and form a coalition, called the Grand Alliance, in order to come up with standards that were acceptable to the FCC. The coalition did so, and the FCC adopted them in 1996. The new standards called for an

ASPECT RATIO

Aspect ratio is the width of the television screen compared to the height, expressed by two numbers separated by a colon. The SD (standard definition) aspect ratio 4:3 means that for every 4 units of width there will be 3 units of height. The HD (high definition) aspect ratio of 16:9 means for every 16 units of width there will be 9 units of height.

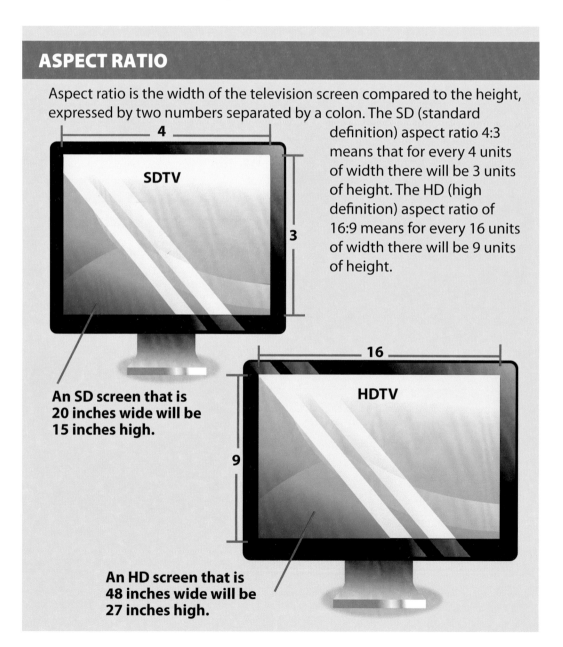

An SD screen that is 20 inches wide will be 15 inches high.

An HD screen that is 48 inches wide will be 27 inches high.

aspect ratio of 16:9 and screen resolution up to 1,920 pixels by 1,080 pixels.

General Instrument was a major supplier of cable television equipment. Two scientists in their San Diego, California, division—Jerrold Heller and Woo Paik—came up with a solution to what had seemed an insurmountable problem. They developed a procedure to compress a full HDTV signal so that it could fit into a 6 megahertz broadcast channel. Heller and Paik's work was instrumental in developing the HDTV system that was eventually approved by the FCC.

Not everyone, however, was enamored with the prospect of high-definition TV. Nicholas Negroponte, director of the MIT Media Lab, said, "Some people think the next revolutionary step in television is high-definition. That is a lot of rubbish. That is silly. If you walk down the street and ask somebody what's wrong with television, you're not going to find anybody who says: Resolution."[38]

Digital Television and High-Definition Television

The technology decided upon to compress the data required for digital picture and sound had been used by personal computers for years. It is known as MPEG-2 (Moving Picture Experts Group). MPEG-2 technology takes advantage of the fact that many pixels in an image remain the same for several frames. Rather than reproducing every one of the thousands of pixels on every high-definition screen, it only records the pixels that change from frame to frame. This results in a tremendous reduction in the amount of data that has to be transmitted.

Because of the reduced space needed for digital signals, broadcasters can add other information within the same bandwidth. Several standard-definition signals can be sent in the same amount of space, as well as assorted services such as subscription television programming, teletext (text-based information such as news, weather and TV schedules), and interactive services. In order to take advantage of the advances

Inside a Television Screen

Television pictures are created on the screen in one of two ways. Standard televisions use a method called interlaced scanning. The picture contains 480 lines of pixels, each of which takes one-sixtieth of a second to draw. Although the National Television Standards Committee standards include pictures drawn with 525 lines, only 480 are actually used in producing the image. Cathode ray tubes require an interval of time to reset the electronic beam to the top of the screen for the next scan. To allow for this, a "vertical blanking interval" equal to 45 lines is incorporated. The total number of lines in each frame is therefore 525 (480 for the picture plus the 45 for the blanking interval). Other information, such as closed-captioning, may be transmitted in this gap.

In interlaced scanning, the odd-numbered lines are drawn first, followed by the even-numbered lines. Each full picture, therefore, takes one-thirtieth of a second to be drawn.

Some digital television standards call for another procedure known as progressive scanning. In this method, the entire picture—including both odd- and even-numbered lines—is scanned in one pass over the screen.

Progressive scanning results in a sharper image, particularly when motion is involved. With interlaced scanning, the image might change position slightly in the fraction of a second between the odd- and even-numbered line scans. This causes what is known as stair-step edges on the moving object. This is not a problem in progressive scanning since the entire image is drawn in one scan.

possible with digital television, it is necessary to have television that can display these signals. This led to the emergence of larger television screens based on new technologies

Flatscreen TVs

Flat panel displays date back to the early 1950s. The first thin cathode ray tube was invented by William Ross Aiken. It was developed for use by the armed forces in airplanes and helicopters. Flat panel displays exploded in popularity with the arrival of digital television.

Liquid crystal display (LCD) televisions were the first ones with HDTV capabilities, followed soon after by plasma televisions. LCD sets contain a pair of transparent polarized glass

panels with a liquid crystal solution between them. When light is shined from behind the panels, the crystals either allow light to pass through or block it. The pattern of crystals forms the image on the screen. In a plasma television the screen is composed of two thin panels of glass that are comprised of thousands of tiny pixel cells of compressed gas. When an electric current is applied, the gas reacts and produces light.

Both LCD and plasma sets are much slimmer and lighter than cathode ray televisions with similar-size screens. Supporters of LCD sets claim they are brighter than plasma sets, with less-reflective screens. Plasma sets are better at producing deep blacks and have better contrast. Although there are benefits and drawbacks to each, LCDs have surged ahead of plasma sets in sales.

DVR Technology

Another advantage of digital television is an improvement in recording and storing television programs. The introduction of the digital video recorder (DVR) in the late 1990s gave the television viewer more control than ever over how and when programs can be watched. VCRs record programs on tape for future viewing. DVRs take the next step by changing television signals into a form that can be stored

As the name implies, digital video recorders (DVRs) record programs digitally instead of to a tape like a VCR. The benefits to viewers are no tapes to keep track of, and a program can be watched while it is still recording.

in what is basically a hard drive. The programs can then be watched at a future time. Because a program is stored as digital signals, there is no tape to worry about. This makes it easier to use than a VCR, but the amount of storage space available is limited.

The main benefit of the DVR is the control it allows for playing back programs. There is no tape to rewind, so a viewer does not have to wait for a program to finish before watching it. The DVR has a buffer, or storage area, which can usually hold about an hour of programming. If a person wants to begin watching a program that is already in progress, he or she can do so by accessing the data stored in the buffer.

DVRs also have a variety of search tools that let the user find the programs he or she wants to record. The "wish list" feature, for example, allows someone to search for programs starring a particular actor or those with a certain word in the title. The "season pass" feature allows the user to record all episodes of a particular show.

For those who prefer watching recordings on their computer, there are programs available that let viewers use the hard drive on their computer as a DVR.

Multichannel Audio

Ever since the 1950s, television makers have taken steps to bring the ultimate in listening experiences into the home. Today's multichannel audio is a far cry from the monophonic systems of the past. The first televisions came with monophonic, single-channel sound. All elements of the sound were emitted from one amplifier and speaker combination, from the same point in space. Two-channel recordings and a second speaker made the sound stereophonic. The first television program broadcast with stereo audio was *The Tonight Show Starring Johnny Carson* on July 26, 1984.

Adding even more channels enables the sound to come from three or more directions, totally enveloping the listener. For example, 5.1 channel systems are common in home theater setups. Five separate speakers decode signals from

TV Turnoff Week

For years people complained about the negative effects of watching too much television. In 1994 Henry Labalme and Matt Pawa decided to do something about it. They formed a nonprofit organization called TV-Free America, later to become the TV-Turnoff Network and then the Center for Screen-Time Awareness (CSTA). Their intention was to raise awareness about the negative effects of watching television and to encourage people to become more involved in other activities.

Toward this end, the two friends instituted TV Turnoff Week in 1995. They asked Americans to unplug, or turn off, their televisions for seven days and substitute that viewing time with other activities, such as reading, playing a musical instrument, participating in a sport, or becoming involved in the community. Participation in the event has grown through the years, and many organizations now support it. These include the National Education Association, the American Medical Association, and the President's Council on Fitness, Sports & Nutrition.

According to CSTA, the events were a great success. Follow-up surveys show 90 percent of responding participants claim to have reduced their time watching television. The percentage of children under the age of twelve who have limits on their viewing time has risen from 63 percent to 72 percent since 2003.

around the room, in addition to a separate low-frequency speaker called a subwoofer.

With the advent of digital television, surround sound has become even clearer and sharper. Like video signals, audio signals are encoded as strings of zeroes and ones. Because this encoding does not degrade as easily as analog signals, none of it is lost in transit. Digital signals can also carry much more detail than analog signals because of the manner in which they are compressed.

The V-Chip

For years the amount of sex, violence, and strong language in television programs has increased, causing a great deal of concern among parents. As more and more channels became available, it became a bigger problem than ever before. In an effort to help parents protect their children, President Bill Clinton signed the Telecommunications Reform Act of 1996. One of the provisions of the act calls for the inclusion of V-chip technology in all televisions manufactured as of January 2000.

Professor Tim Collings of Simon Fraser University is usually credited with having invented the V-chip in the early 1990s. Although Collings said the V stood for "viewer" choice, it has come to be associated with violence on television. The chip works by reading a code that is embedded when a program is transmitted. The code indicates the rating that has been given to the program. Parents can program a television with the V-chip to block all shows above a particular rating. The rating appears for fifteen seconds at the beginning of all rated shows.

The V-chip ratings system was developed to guide viewers on the content of television programming. The ratings are intended to help parents screen appropriate shows for their children.

Reaction to the V-Chip

Not all reactions to the use of V-chip technology were positive. The television networks opposed the idea on grounds that blocking programs violated the First Amendment right to freedom of speech. The networks argued that a person did not have to watch something he or she considered inappropriate and that no one should have the right to decide for others if the content of a program is too violent or suggestive. The networks really opposed the V-chip because they were worried about losing revenue. Sponsors would be hesitant about spending money for commercial time on programs that might be blocked.

Others questioned how effective the V-chip would actually be. One such person was Leonard Eron, an adjunct professor at the University of Michigan who had done research on the causes of violent behavior in children. Eron says, "It's a step in the right direction, but a parent has to be concerned, and has to be available to do it. The V-chip will have some effect, but it doesn't solve the problem, not with two working parents, single-parent families and, frankly, a lot of parents who don't give a darn."[39]

Eron appears to have been right. Only a small percentage of parents actually use the V-chip. A 2007 survey reports that only 15 percent of those who had access to the chip actually use it. About 20 percent of parents surveyed decided not to use it, while 39 percent were unaware that their sets included one.

TV Ratings

The TV ratings system is a tool to help parents determine which programs are acceptable for their children to watch. All programs—except news, sports, and unedited movies on premium cable channels—receive a rating that appears in the upper left corner of the screen during the first fifteen seconds of each program. The ratings are:

- TV-Y: Appropriate for children ages two to six.

- TV-Y7: Appropriate for children ages seven and up.
- TV-Y7-FV: May contain fantasy violence too intense for young children.
- TV-G: Appropriate for general audiences (all ages).
- TV-PG: May be unsuitable for young children and parental guidance is suggested. The rating may include a V for violence, S for sexual situations, L for language, or D for suggestive dialogue.
- TV-14: May be unsuitable for children under fourteen. May also include a rating of V, S, L, or D.
- TV-MA: For mature audiences only (ages seventeen and up). Programs may contain violence, sexual situations, profane language and/or suggestive dialogue.

Movie ratings assigned by a parents' board known as the Classification and Rating Administration are also programmed into the V-chip. These ratings are:

- G: Appropriate for all ages.
- PG: May be unsuitable for young children and parental guidance is suggested.
- PG-13: Contains material that may be inappropriate for children under thirteen.
- R: Contains material that may be inappropriate for children under seventeen. Admission to movies with this rating is restricted. Children under seventeen are only admitted if accompanied by a parent or guardian who is seventeen or older.
- NC-17: Contains material considered inappropriate for children under eighteen. Admission to movies with this rating is restricted. No one under eighteen years of age is admitted.

CHAPTER 5

Into the Future

P hilo Farnsworth could never have imagined how far technology would progress in the eighty-plus years since his first success with electrical television in 1928. In the same way, it may be hard to imagine what television will be like through the twenty-first century. If current research is any indication, however, it will likely be more interactive, more lifelike, and even easier to use than it is today.

Gesture-Controlled Television

Gesture-controlled technology can be seen in the 2002 movie *Minority Report*. The main character, played by Tom Cruise, moves items around on his computer by waving his hands. It was not long after that Nintendo came out with the Wii video game console, in which users employ a gestural interface and a wireless remote to control actions on the screen. The controller contains components that lets it sense a variety of movements. These include tilting and rotation up and down and left and right; rotation along the main axis; and acceleration up and down, left and right, and toward and away from the screen.

Gesture-controlled television is currently being developed by several manufacturers. These televisions will

A boy plays a tennis game on the Wii game system. Gesture-controlled technology is quickly being developed and will continue to change the way viewers interact with their television screens.

enable the user to turn the set off and on, switch channels, adjust volume, and scroll through menus by using a series of predefined movements of the hand. Jim Spare, chief executive officer of chipmaker Canesta, says, "It's great that you don't have to hunt for the remote, but the real impact of 3-D natural interfaces, such as gesture controlled TVs, is that they will make a broad array of complex services

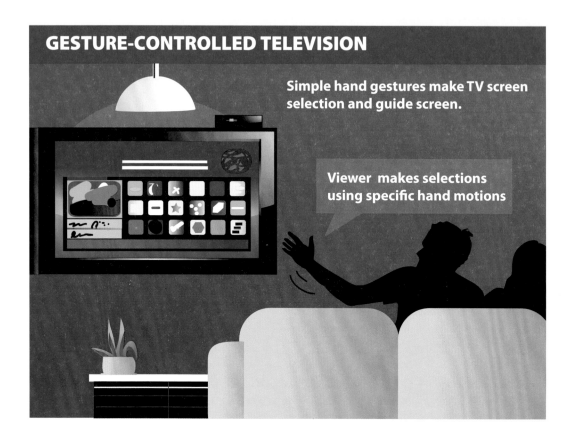

GESTURE-CONTROLLED TELEVISION

Simple hand gestures make TV screen selection and guide screen.

Viewer makes selections using specific hand motions

easily available and accessible through a very natural user experience."[40]

Organic Light-Emitting Diode Technology

Since flatscreen televisions first came out, plasma and LCD screens have dominated the market. Organic light-emitting diode (OLED) technology, however, may well be the wave of the future. In OLEDs, a series of organic films are placed between two transparent electrodes. When an electric current is applied, bright light is produced. The OLED panels are extremely thin and use little electrical current. Because of their thinness, the panels can even be rolled up. Sony spokesman Chisato Kitsukawa says, "In the future, it could get wrapped around a lamppost or a person's wrist, even worn as clothing. Perhaps it can be put up like wallpaper."[41]

In addition to their flexibility, OLEDs have other characteristics that would make them ideal for HDTV. They are brighter than LCDs because they are emissive, rather than transmissive, devices. This means they emit, or give off, light instead of transmitting it from a light source behind the screen. It is the same process found in nature in fireflies and plankton. OLEDs are also more durable and use less power than other screens, making them more environmentally friendly. The biggest disadvantage with OLEDs is the high cost of producing them. As with other new technologies, however, the cost will come down as production methods improve.

3-D Television

Many television industry insiders believe that 3-D television is the next "big thing" on the horizon. This technology has been around since the first public demonstration of 3-D movies in New York City in 1915. Three short movies, called shorts, made by Edwin S. Porter and William E. Waddell were shown for an audience at the Astor Theater. Two camera lenses spaced inches apart, like human eyes, filmed the action. The movies were projected onto a screen through a pair of projectors, one with a red filter and the other with a green one. The audience wore glasses with one red and one green lens (anaglyphs) so that each eye saw a slightly different image, giving the impression of depth. The effect was fairly primitive and not very impressive. As a reviewer for *Moving Picture World* magazine reported, "Images shimmered like reflections on a lake and in its present form the method couldn't be commercial because it detracts from the plot."[42]

3-D Movie Technology

The use of tinted lenses in the glasses the audience wore for the movies shown in 1915 interfered with true color clarity. Inventor Edwin Land came up with a solution to this problem in the 1930s. It involved polarization. In polarization, two images are projected onto a screen made of a reflective material. Rather than particular colors, however, polarized glasses filter out light rays that are projected at a particular angle. Each eye sees only one set of images on the screen, as with anaglyphs, but the color is truer.

The technology continued to improve over the years, but 3-D movies remained a novelty. By the 1950s television had gained in popularity and attendance in theaters had dropped. In an effort to attract more customers, the movie industry again turned to 3-D. This time, their efforts were more successful. The 1953 Warner Bros. film *House of Wax*, starring Vincent Price, was the first 3-D feature film with stereophonic sound. Its success sparked a 3-D boom, but the fad did not last long. People complained that 3-D caused eyestrain, while others objected to having to wear 3-D glasses.

Since that time, the technology has gotten more sophisticated and 3-D has had several revivals. The IMAX 3-D format is the latest and most significant improvement. Shooting costs are still prohibitive, however, and it is only used in specialized productions.

Having to wear special glasses still makes viewing awkward. Tom Huntington summarized 3-D's status in a 2003 article for *American Heritage* magazine, writing, "As long as 3-D remains a cumbersome and intermittent sideshow, it will have a hard time establishing itself as a legitimate tool of cinematic art."[43]

A New 3-D Technology

BITS & BYTES

$3,200

Average cost of a 3-D-ready HDTV in 2010

In the mid-1970s, engineers came up with a new method for creating three-dimensional images. It was not until 2009, however, that it was adapted for use with modern flatscreen TVs. In it, the user wears glasses that have liquid crystal display (LCD) lenses that play an active role in the process. Two sets of images are projected on the screen,

but the picture alternates between the two at a rapid speed. As the images alternate on the screen, the left and right lens of the glasses alternately open and close. Panasonic's Keisuke Suetsugi explains, "When the TV is showing the left image, the shutter closes the right eye so people can see only the left image. And the next moment, when the TV is showing the right image, the shutter glass is covering the left."[44]

Unfortunately, until relatively recently, LCD and plasma television screens did not have a high enough refresh rate (the speed at which the picture is renewed on the screen) to take advantage of the new technology. Newer 3-D-ready televisions can do so. They come with a special port for a stereoscopic sync signal connector that connects with an emitter that sends signals to the glasses.

3-D movie technology, such as that used in the popular 2009 movie Avatar, *has been part of an occasional yet usually short-lived fad throughout movie history.*

Autostereoscopic Television

Although shutter glasses provide a better picture than the earlier red-and-green lens technology, two problems still remain: The glasses are unwieldy and expensive, and content on the screen cannot be viewed without the glasses. Autostereoscopic television may eliminate these problems. Autostereoscopic television is television that can produce three-dimensional pictures without the use of any additional equipment, like glasses or headbands. The two main technologies currently being developed involve the use of lenticular lenses and parallax barrier.

The first method employs tiny cylindrical plastic lenses called lenticules. The lenticules are arranged on a transparent sheet that is fixed onto the surface of a screen. Each of the tiny lenses magnifies the part of the image underneath it. Each eye of the viewer sees a slightly different image since it sees the screen from a different angle.

The main problem with lenticular lenses is that viewers must sit in a precise spot a specific distance from the screen in order to get the 3-D effect. When viewed from any other position, the images appear jumbled. One way of getting around this problem is to have a processor in the set generate more than two views. This would allow the viewer to move around without any image distortion.

The parallax barrier technology works on a similar principle. Instead of being covered with tiny lenses, the screen is covered with a layer on which tiny slits are arranged. When switched on, the barrier controls how and where the light leaves the display, again giving the eyes two slightly different views. One benefit of the parallax barrier is that it is the only technology that can also provide a flat, two-dimensional image when the barrier is switched off.

Many industry observers believe the biggest obstacle facing 3-D television is the content issue. That is, other than some movies, there are very few programs produced in 3-D. In addition, there are other obstacles. Broadcasts using the newer technologies are much more expensive to produce.

How the Eye Works

Human beings see things in three dimensions because they have two eyes side by side. Since the eyes are positioned about 2 inches (5cm) apart, each one sees a slightly different image from a slightly different angle when a person views an object. The images are sent to the brain which processes the two, merging them into a single image. The difference between the two images is what gives the impression of depth. The result is what appears as a three-dimensional stereo image (the word *stereo* comes from the Greek word *stereos*, meaning "firm" or "solid"). In 3-D television and movies, each eye is shown a slightly different picture—or the same picture from a slightly different angle—tricking the brain into thinking that the image has depth.

Edwin Herbert Land

Edwin Herbert Land's work with polarization was crucial to the development of modern 3-D technology. He is best remembered today, however, for his invention of instant photography.

Soon after World War II, Land began work on an instantaneous developing film that would eventually lead to a system of one-step photography. He was inspired by his three-year-old daughter, who asked him why she could not see photos he had taken right away.

In Land's original system, the photographer first took a reading of the light level, then set the exposure. The picture that was taken was recorded directly onto a photosensitive surface. The negative was pulled over the positive through rollers that spread the developing agent. After waiting for the picture to develop inside the camera, the photographer peeled the positive away from the negative to reveal the photo.

Land's Polaroid Model 95 camera went on the market in November 1948. It was named for its suggested retail price of ninety-five dollars, the equivalent of over eight hundred dollars today. Land made improvements to his camera over the years, coming out with an automatic exposure camera in 1960 and the first color Polaroid film three years later.

More cameras are needed to record the shows, and more bandwidth is needed to present them. Steve Hellmuth, executive vice president of technology and operations for the National Basketball Association, says, "Transporting live, high-definition 3D streams is very expensive. So there has to be sufficient demand and a pool of content before satellite and cable operators will devote resources to delivering it."[45]

Holograms

A hologram is a true three-dimensional image. Hungarian physicist Dennis Gabor, the father of holography, coined the word in 1947. It comes from the Greek *holos*, meaning "whole," and *gramma*, meaning "message." A hologram reproduces everything that your eyes see from a variety of different angles. If you move your head around while looking at it, you see the image from different viewpoints.

To produce a hologram, lasers copy the way light waves reflect off an object onto a light-sensitive film or other

surface. The film is then developed and again exposed to a light. The result is an image with all the characteristics of the original object, including size, depth, shape, and texture. Holograms are grouped into two main categories: reflection and transmission. A reflection hologram is lit from the front and reflects the light to the person viewing it. A transmission hologram is lit from the rear. Light passes through it to the viewer's eyes.

Holograms, such as those portrayed in the Star Wars *movie series, may eventually come into people's living rooms as technology continues to change.*

Holographic Video

In a famous scene from the movie *Star Wars*, a hologram of Princess Leia sends a message to Obi-Wan Kenobi. Thanks to the work of Harold Garner of the University of Texas Southwestern Medical Center, that technology may eventually be used in homes. In 2003 Garner and his team of engineers built a machine that generated holographic movies. The first was a grainy red clip of circling fighter jets.

At the heart of Garner's system is a computer chip covered with almost one million tiny reflective mirrors. A computer changes the angle of the mirrors thousands of times a second as laser light reflects off them. Developing a suitable screen has been a challenge. One possibility is a display composed of layers of microthin LCD panels. When charged, the panels become either clear or opaque. If done rapidly, this can produce the impression of movement.

Another problem is the enormous amount of data needed to produce the image. An event would have to be recorded by a series of cameras shooting from all sides, with the images incorporated into a single image that would be projected on a screen. This would require high-speed processing and advanced techniques for data compression in order for it to be handled by television channels.

Holographic applications are ideally suited for use in the medical and military fields, as well as in gaming and television. Phillip Swann, president and publisher of TV Predictions .com, believes the results will be spectacular. While addressing the 2004 PBS Technology Conference in Las Vegas, Nevada, Swann said, "In the next 15 years, Hologram TV will permit images to float from your TV screen directly into your living room. . . . Viewers will have more difficulty separating fact from fiction. When you see a character shoot someone in your living room, you will ask, 'Did it really happen? Or, did I watch it on TV.'"[46]

Interactive Commercials

Interactive commercials are commercials in which viewers can order brochures, coupons, samples or products by clicking a button on their television remote during the commercial. They have been in development for several years, with Cablevision making them available for use on a trial basis in late 2009. Paint company Benjamin Moore signed up as one of its first customers.

In the future, viewers will be able to buy products that appear in programs in a similar way. They will be able to purchase an outfit worn by an actress, for example, by clicking a button on the remote when she appears on the screen.

Advertisers will be able to aim messages at specific audiences. Dog owners might be asked to push a button to view more dog-friendly ads. By using personal data kept on subscribers by cable companies, advertisers will be able to target their audiences even more. A commercial for a luxury car can be shown to viewers in an upper-class neighborhood, while those living in a middle-class area see one for a family sedan. Families with young children will be exposed to commercials aimed at that particular age group while senior citizen viewers will not. Such targeted advertising, however, would raise privacy questions because of the personal data being used.

Interactivity and Content

Television technology is not the only thing that will change in the coming years. Viewer interaction has increased significantly from 2000 to 2010. On-screen menus and listing guides, on-demand services, and Internet TV allow users to see what they want, when they want it. Viewers will even be able to influence what happens on the screen. An example can be found in the Finnish interactive musical comedy series, *Accidental Lovers*. By sending mobile text messages to the broadcast, viewers can transform the plot on the basis of keywords used in the messages.

Many observers believe television and the Internet will merge in the future. This will lead to even more interactivity between the viewer and the content he or she wants to see. Watching a video posted on a Web site, for example, could be viewed on the television.

Television will likely then become a gateway to the Internet. Instead of using a computer to check e-mail or send instant messages, people will use their televisions. It may be

Viewers will likely interact with their televisions much differently in the future, as interactive menus allow specific content to be pulled up and Internet access via the TV becomes more common.

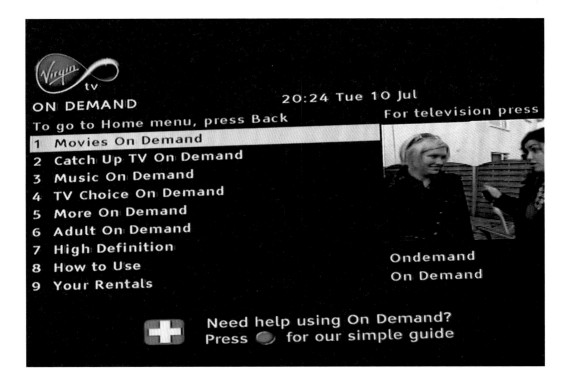

possible to chat with a friend while watching the same show and have the chat conversation appear on the screen along with the television program. Of course, this would require changing the configuration of TV remotes. Future remotes will likely have touch screens or keyboards like modern cell phones.

This, in turn, would lead to even more interaction. While watching a movie, users could ask for a biography of the handsome new lead actor, or information on the car he's driving. Programs might conduct online polls, asking viewers questions about the show they are watching as it appears before them. This could even lead to online voting during award programs, where winners would truly be the "viewer's choice."

Screen Interaction

The ultimate form of interaction may come through the television screen itself. Screens will be made that can identify who is watching at any particular moment. Stan Glasgow, president and chief operating officer of Sony Electronics Inc., says, "I think we are going to be able to interact with voice and movement. We're going to be able to recognize who is watching the set by their eyes and change parental controls automatically."[47] Such screens will be able to skip past scenes in a program that contain sex and violence if the viewer is below a certain age level. They will also be able to optimize the viewing experience in other ways. By sensing how far a viewer is from the screen, the television will be able to adjust the size of the image accordingly. It may even be possible to offer viewers a choice of viewing angles while watching a program.

Advances such as these may appear to be in the realm of science fiction. With improvements in technology coming at a rapid rate, however, they may be here in the very near future. Even more unimaginable things may lurk on the distant horizon. Perhaps, for example, people will control television with their minds and remote controls will no longer be needed.

Whatever the future may bring, one thing is certain: Television will still be with us in one form or another. Whether it enriches daily life or simply wastes time depends entirely on how it is used. As radio and television news correspondent Edward R. Murrow once said, "the instrument can teach, it can illuminate, yes and it can even inspire. But it can only do so to the extent that humans are determined to use it to those ends. Otherwise, it is merely wires and lights in a box."[48]

Introduction: A Modern Miracle

1. Quoted in Michael Roney. "Microsoft Driving Next Generation of TV Experiences." Forbes Custom .com, www.forbescustom.com/ TelecomPgs/IPTVP2.html.
2. Quoted in Finest Quotes. "Groucho Marx Quotes." Finest Quotes, www .finestquotes.com/author_quotes- author-groucho%20marx-page-0 .htm.
3. Quoted in Quotation Vault .com. "Paddy Chayevsky Quotations." Quotation Vault.com, www .quotationvault.com/author/ paddy_chayevsky.

Chapter 1: Inventing the Technology

4. Quoted in Prof. Angel Lozano. "The Hall of Innovation." Prof. Angel Lozano (website), www.dtic.upf .edu/~alozano/innovation.
5. Quoted in Peter Baida. "Hindsight, Foresight, and No Sight." American Heritage, June–July 1985.www .americanheritage.com/articles/ magazine/ah/1985/4/1985_4_18_ print.shtml.

6. Quoted in Barbara Roisman Cooper. "John Logie Baird: Forgotten Pioneer of Television." British Heritage, February 1, 2005, www.historynet .com/john-logie-baird-forgotten- pioneer-of-television.htm.
7. Quoted in David E. Fisher and Marshall Jon Fisher. Tube: The Invention of Television, Washington, DC: Counterpoint, 1996, p. 34.
8. Quoted in Fisher and Fisher. Tube, pp. 38–39.
9. Quoted in Robert McG. Thomas Jr. "Vladimir Zworykin, Television Pioneer, Dies at 92." New York Times, August 1, 1982, www .nytimes.com/1982/08/01/ obituaries/vladimir-zworykin- television-pioneer-dies-at-92.html.
10. Quoted in Fisher and Fisher. Tube, p. 173.
11. Quoted in Thomas. "Vladimir Zworykin, Television Pioneer, Dies at 92."
12. Quoted in Neil Postman. "The TIME 100: Scientists & Thinkers: Philo Farnsworth." Time, March 29, 1999, http://205.188.238.109/ time/time100/scientist/profile/ farnsworth02.html.
13. San Francisco Chronicle. "S.F. Man's Invention to Revolutionize

Television." *San Francisco Chronicle*, September 3, 1928, www.sfmuseum.org/hist10/philo.html.

14. Quoted in Fisher and Fisher. *Tube*, p. 191.

15. Quoted in Fisher and Fisher. *Tube*, p. 212.

16. Quoted in Gerald Parshall. "Philo T. Farnsworth: 'Dr. X's' Instant Images." *U.S. News & World Report*, August 17, 1998, www.usnews.com/usnews/culture/articles/980817/archive_004567.htm.

Chapter 2: The Networks Take Control

17. Quoted in AT&T. "History of AT&T and Television." AT&T (Web site), www.corp.att.com/history/television.

18. Quoted in Fisher and Fisher. *Tube*, p. 278.

19. Quoted in J. Fred MacDonald. *One Nation Under Television*, Chicago, IL: Nelson-Hall, 1994, www.jfredmacdonald.com/onutv/battle.htm.

20. Quoted in MacDonald. *One Nation Under Television*, www.jfredmacdonald.com/onutv/publicissues.htm.

21. Quoted in MacDonald. *One Nation Under Television*, www.jfredmacdonald.com/onutv/arrival.htm.

22. Quoted in Fisher and Fisher. *Tube*, pp. 305–306.

23. Quoted in Fisher and Fisher. *Tube*, p. 307.

24. Quoted in MacDonald. *One Nation Under Television*, www.jfredmacdonald.com/onutv/postwar.htm.

25. Jack Gould. "Time for a Halt." *New York Times*, July 16, 1950.

26. Quoted in Keisha L. Hoerrner. "The Forgotten Battles: Congressional Hearings on Television Violence in the 1950s." *Web Journal of Mass Communication Research*, June 1999, www.scripps.ohiou.edu/wjmcr/vol02/2-3a-B.htm.

27. Quoted in MacDonald. *One Nation Under Television*, www.jfredmacdonald.com/onutv/profanity.htm.

28. Quoted in Christine Rosen. "The Age of Egocasting." *New Atlantis*, Fall 2004–Winter 2005, pp. 51–72. Also available online at www.thenewatlantis.com/publications/the-age-of-egocasting.

29. Newton Minow. "Television and the Public Interest" speech, annual convention of the National Association of Broadcasters, Washington, DC, May 9, 1961, www.americanrhetoric.com/speeches/newtonminow.htm.

Chapter 3: A Variety of Choices

30. Quoted in Gary R. Edgerton. *The Columbia History of American Television*, New York: Columbia University Press, 2007, p. 302.

31. Quoted in Imagining the Internet. "1920s–1960s Television."

Imagining the Internet (website), www.elon.edu/e-web/predictions/150/1930.xhtml.

32. Henry Louis Gates Jr. "TV's Black World Turns—But Stays Unreal." *New York Times*, November 12, 1989, www.nytimes.com/1989/11/12/arts/tv-s-black-world-turns-but-stays-unreal.html?pagewanted=all.

33. Quoted in Alexander B. Magoun. *Television: The Life Story of a Technology*, Westport, CT: Greenwood Technographies, 2007, p. 128.

34. Ralph Baer. "Genesis: How the Home Video Games Industry Began." www.ralphbaer.com, www.ralphbaer.com/how_video_games.htm.

Chapter 4: Improving the Product

35. Quoted in Ken Freed. "When Cable Went Qubist." Interactive TV (Web site), www.media-visions.com/itv-qube.html.

36. Quoted in Freed. "When Cable Went Qubist."

37. Quoted in Freed. "When Cable Went Qubist."

38. Quoted in Marc Doyle. *The Future of Television: A Global Overview of Programming, Advertising, Technology, and Growth*, Lincolnwood, IL: NTC Business Books, 1992, p. 165.

39. Quoted in Jeff Mortimer. "Chipping Away at Violence." *Michigan Today*, June 1996, www.ns.umich.edu/MT/96/Jun96/mta14j96.html.

Chapter 5: Into the Future

40. Quoted in *Business Wire*. "3-D Natural Interfaces Will Control a Wide Range of Gear—From PC's to TV's and Much More, Says Canesta CEO." *Business Wire*, November 16, 2009, www.tmcnet.com/usubmit/2009/11/16/4483011.htm.

41. Quoted in Associated Press. "Sony Shows Off Paper-Thin, Bendable Video Display." Associated Press, May 29, 2007, www.foxnews.com/story/0,2933,275514,00.html?sPage=fnc/scitech/innovation.

42. Quoted in Paul Arnett. "See UH in Another Dimension." *Honolulu Star-Bulletin*, September 2, 2005, http://archives.starbulletin.com/2005/09/02/special.

43. Tom Huntington. "The Gimmick That Ate Hollywood." *American Heritage*, Spring 2003, www.americanheritage.com/articles/magazine/it/2003/4/2003_4_34.shtml.

44. Quoted in Colin Parrott. "Coming Soon to the Small Screen: TV in 3D." Reuters, September 29, 2009, www.reuters.com/article/technologynews/idustre58S0v420090929.

45. Quoted in Marguerite Reardon. "3D Is Coming to a Living Room Near You." CNET Ne ws, http://ces.cnet.com/8301-19167_1-10142957-100.html.

46. Quoted in Phillip Swann. "Hologram TV: Better than HDTV?"

TVPredictions.com, April 18, 2007, www.tvpredictions.com/hologramtv041807.htm.

47. Quoted in Jonathan Fildes. "Future Television Switches On." BBC News, January 9, 2008, http://news.bbc.co.uk/2/hi/technology/7178288.stm.

48. Quoted in Harold Evans. "Good Night, and Good Luck." BBC News, October 17, 2005, http://news.bbc.co.uk/2/hi/uk_news/magazine/4343006.stm.

aspect ratio: The ratio of the width to the height of a television picture.

cathode ray tube: A vacuum tube in which images are created when a beam of electrons scans across a phosphor-coated screen.

digital television (DTV): The sending and receiving of moving images by signals that are encoded as strings of zeroes and ones.

high-definition television (HDTV): A digital television format in which a sharper picture can be transmitted due to a larger number of lines per frame.

hologram: A three-dimensional image.

interlaced scan: A method of transmitting pictures in which the even-numbered lines are displayed first, then the odd-numbered lines.

liquid crystal display (LCD): Flatscreen displays that produce pictures by using an electric current to align crystals in a special liquid.

plasma: Flatscreen displays that produce pictures by using gas-filled cells positioned between two transparent glass panels.

progressive scan: A method of transmitting pictures in which all the lines of a frame are displayed in sequence.

resolution: The sharpness of an image.

ultrasonics: Sounds above the frequency range of human hearing.

V-chip: Television component that allows programs to be filtered according to ratings criteria.

FOR MORE INFORMATION

Books

David E. Fisher and Marshall Jon Fisher. *Tube: The Invention of Television.* Washington, DC: Counterpoint, 1996. Excellent history of television, with emphasis on the personalities responsible for one of the century's most significant inventions.

Jeff Kisseloff. *The Box: An Oral History of Television 1929–1961.* New York: Penguin, 1996. An oral history taken from hundreds of interviews with those involved in the invention, manufacture, and production of television through the years.

Alexander B. Magoun. *Television: The Life Story of a Technology.* Westport, CT: Greenwood, 2007. A comprehensive history of television.

Stephanie Sammartino McPherson. *TV's Forgotten Hero: The Story of Philo Farnsworth.* Minneapolis, MN: Carolrhoda, 1996. Juvenile biography of the man generally credited as the inventor of television.

Evan I. Schwartz. *The Last Lone Inventor: A Tale of Genius, Deceit, and the Birth of Television.* New York: Harper, 2003. The story of Philo Farnsworth and his confrontations with David Sarnoff and RCA.

Websites

Center for Media Literacy (www.medialit .org). Contains a comprehensive collection of articles dealing with media issues, including many concerning television.

Federal Communications Commission (www.fcc.gov). This website includes the informative section "Historical Periods in Television Technology."

How Stuff Works (www.howstuffworks .com). Excellent website with articles and videos showing the inner workings of hundreds of everyday inventions and innovations, including many dealing with television technology.

MZTV Museum of Television (www .mztv.com). The official website of the MZTV Museum of Television, located in Toronto, Canada.

Television History (www.tvhistory .tv). Website chronicling the history of television from pre-1935 to 2000. Includes dozens of color pictures of old televisions.

INDEX

A

ABC (American Broadcasting Company), 39
Academy of Television Arts and Sciences, 23
ACATS (Advisory Committee on Advanced Television Service), 75
Adler, Robert, 50
Advanced television service (ATS), 75
Advertising, 96
Advisory Committee on Advanced Television Service (ACATS), 75
African Americans, 60–62
Aiken, William Ross, 78
Ali, Muhammad, 59, *59*
American Broadcasting Company (ABC), 39
Amos 'n' Andy (television show), 60, *61*
Ampex Corporation, 62–63
Antennas, *54*
Aspect ratio, 73–74, 76–77, *76*
Atkinson, George, 66
ATS (advanced television service), 75
AT&T, 55
Audio, 16–19, 81–82
Audion vacuum tubes, 18–19
Autostereoscopic television, 92–94
Avatar (movie), *91*

B

Baer, Ralph, 66
Baird, John Logie, 20–22, 39
Beavis and Butt-Head (animated show), 44
Bell, Alexander Graham, 17
Bell Laboratories, 35
Berzelius, Jöns Jakob, 19
Betamax system, 63–64, *64*
Boxing, 59, *59*
Braun, Ferdinand, 23–25
Broadcast companies
    restructuring, 38–39
    self-regulation, 47–48
    See also specific companies

Broadcasting

    color television, 41–42
    companies, 33
    transmission standards, 72–74
Brown Box, 66

C

Cable television
    government regulation, 56, 58
    Home Box Office (HBO), 54–55
    households with, *57*
    satellite service, 59–60
    signal transmission, 53–54
    Walson, John, 43–44
Cameras, 18, 94
Carey, George R., 18
Carroll, Diahann, 61
Cassyd, Syd, 23
Cathode ray tubes, 23–25, *24*, *26*, 78
CBS (Columbia Broadcasting System)
    Amos 'n' Andy (television show), 60, *61*
    color television, 39–40, *40*, 41
    videotape, 62–63
Center for Screen-Time Awareness (CSTA), 82
Children, 44–46, 58, 84
Chinn, Howard, 62
Civil rights movement, 61
Clinton, Bill, 83
Closed-captioning, 65
Collings, Tim, 83
Color television, 39–42, *40*, *42*
Columbia Broadcasting System (CBS)
    Amos 'n' Andy (television show), 60, *61*
    color television, 39–40, *40*, 41
    videotape, 62–63
Commercials, interactive, 96
Communications satellites, 55–56
Community Antenna Television (CATV).
    See Cable television
Congressional hearings, 45–47, *46*

Content
Congressional hearings, 45–47
industry self-regulation, 47–48
minorities, representation of, 60–62
Minow, Newton, criticism of, 51–52
range of, 12–13
V-chip technology, 82–84
violence, 44–45
Copyright issues, 64–65
Cosby, Bill, 61
Costs
color television, 41–42
early television sets, 37–38, *37*
QUBE system, 70
remote controls, 50
Court cases, 64–65
Criticism
content, 44–45
Minow, Newton, 51–52
negative impact of television, 14
sedentary lifestyle, television's contribution to, 48
stereotypes, 60
Culture, 60–62

D
Data compression, 77
De Forest, Lee, 18–19
Dickson, W.K.L., 74
Digital television, 71–72, 74–78, *75*
Digital video recorders (DVRs), 80–81, *80*
Disk-based technology, 19–23, *26*
Dolan, Charles, 55
DVRs (digital video recorders), 80–81, *80*

E
Educational programs, 13
Electromagnetic waves, 18
Emmy Awards, 23
England, 20–22
Eron, Leonard, 84

F
Fair-use doctrine, 65
Farnsworth, Philo Taylor, 28–32, *30*
Federal Communications Commission (FCC)
Advisory Committee on Advanced Television Service (ACATS), 75
cable television, 56, 58
color television, 41
Communications Act, 35

program content, 47
satellites, 59
transmission standards, 72–74
Federal Radio Commission (FRC), 34
First Amendment rights, 84
Flash-Matic remote control, 50
Flatscreen televisions, 78–80, *79*
Fly, James Lawrence, 39
Frazier, Joe, 59, *59*
FRC (Federal Radio Commission), 34
Future of technology
certainty of television's presence, 99
gesture-controlled television, 86–88
holography, 94–96
interactive television, 96–98
organic light-emitting diode technology, 88–89
3-D, 89–94

G
Gabor, Dennis, 94
Games, 66–67, *67, 87*
Garner, Harold, 95
Gathings, E.C., 45
Gesture-controlled television, 86–88, *87, 88*
Ginsburg, Charles, 62
Glasses for 3-D viewing, 90–92, *92*
Goldmark, Peter, 39–40
Government regulation
cable television, 56, 58
history, 34–35
industry standards, 38, 72–74, *75–77*
radio network restructuring, 38–39
satellites, 59
Grand Alliance, 75–76
Green Channel, 55

H
Harris, Oren, 45, *46*
HBO (Home Box Office), 54–55, 59–60, *59*
Health issues, 48, 58
Hearings, congressional, 45–47
Heller, Jerrold, 77
High-definition television, 74–78, *75*
Hispanic Americans, 62
History
Emmy Awards, 23
forecast of television's impact, 10

History (Cont.)
    government regulation, 34–35
    technological improvements, 10–12
    telegraphy, 16–17
Holography, 94–96, *95*
Home Box Office (HBO), 54–55, 59–60, *59*
Home videocassette recorders, 63–66
Hoover, Herbert, 35
Households with cable television, *57*
Hytron, 41

I
Image dissector, 29–31
Industry self-regulation, 47–48, 83–85
Industry standards, 38, 72 77
Infrared technology, 51
Interactive television, 68–70, *69*, 96,
    97–98, *97*
Interlaced scanning, 78
Internet television, 70–71, *71*, 97–98, *97*
Inventions
    cathode ray tubes, 23–25
    color television, 39–42
    HDTV signal compression, 77
    holographic video, 95
    interactive television, 68–70
    Nipkow disks, 19–20
    Polaroid camera, 94
    radio, 17–19
    "radiovision," 22
    remote controls, 48–51
    selenium cameras, 18
    telegraphy, 16–17
    "televisor," 20–22
    thin cathode ray tubes, 78
    V-chip technology, 82–83
    video games, 66–67
    videotape recorders, 62–63
Inventors
    Adler, Robert, 50
    Baer, Ralph, 66
    Baird, John Logie, 20–22, 39
    Bell, Alexander Graham, 17
    Berzelius, Jöns Jakob, 19
    Braun, Ferdinand, 23–25
    Carey, George R., 18
    Collings, Tim, 83
    De Forest, Lee, 18–19
    Farnsworth, Philo Taylor, 28–32

    Ginsburg, Charles, 62
    Goldmark, Peter, 39–40
    Heller, Jerrold, 77
    Jenkins, Charles Francis, 22–23
    Land, Edwin, 89–90, 94
    Marconi, Guglielmo, 18
    Mose, Samuel, 16–17
    Nipkow, Paul, 19–20
    Paik, Woo, 77
    Polley, Eugene, 50
    Swinton, A.A. Campbell, 25
    Tesla, Nikola, 48–49
    Zworykin, Vladimir, 25–28

J
Japan Broadcasting Corporation, 74–75
Jenkins, Charles Francis, 22
Juvenile delinquency, 46

K
Kennedy, John F., *56*

L
Labalme, Henry, 82
Land, Edwin, 89–90, 94
Lawsuits, 64–65
Lazy Bones remote control, 50
LCD (liquid crystal display) technology, 78–80
Legal issues, 64–65
Legislation
    Radio Act of 1927, 34
    Telecommunications Reform Act, 83
    Television Decoder Circuitry Act, 65
Lenticular lenses, 92–93
Levin, Gerald, 55, 60
Licensing, 32, 34
Line installer and repairer, 47
Liquid crystal display (LCD) technology, 78–80

M
Magnavox Odyssey system, 66
Marconi, Guglielmo, *17*, 18
Maxwell, James Clerk, 17–18
May, Joseph, 19
Microwaves, 53–54
Minorities, 60–62
Minow, Newton, 51–52
Morse, Samuel, 16–17
Movies, 3-D, 89–90, 91
MPEG-2 technology, 77

MTV, 44
Multichannel audio, 81–82
MUSE. *See* High-definition television

N

National Broadcasting Company (NBC)
  color television, 42
  formation of, 27
  programming, 36
News media, 13
1950s television, *11*
Nintendo Wii, 67, *87*
Nipkow disks, 19–20, *26*
Nipkow, Paul, 19–20
Nippon Hoso Kyokai, 74–75

O

Occupations
  telecommunications line installer and
    repairer, 47
  television repairpersons, 72
Organic light-emitting diode (OLED)
  technology, 88–89

P

Paik, Woo, 77
Patents and patent applications
  Farnsworth, Philo Taylor, 29, 30–32
  remote controls, 48
  Zworykin, Vladimir, 25–26
Pawa, Matt, 82
Pay-per-view, 69
Persistence of vision, 20
Perskyi, Constantin, 16
Phantom Teleceiver, 35
Philco, 30, 49
Philips, 63
Photography, 94
Pixels, 73, *73*
Plasma televisions, 80
Polarization, 90, 94
Polley, Eugene, 50
Prinze, Freddie, 62
Programming
  color television, 41–42
  industry self-regulation, 47–48
  NBC, 36
  violence, 44–45
Progressive scanning, 78
Psychological issues, 44–45

Q

QUBE system, 68–70

R

Radio, *34*
  government regulation, 34
  invention of, 17–19
  restructuring of networks, 38–39
Radio Act of 1927, 34
Radio Corporation of America (RCA)
  color television, 40–41
  early television costs, 37–38
  patent challenge, 31–32
  Sarnoff, David, 27–28
  World's Fair exhibit, 35, 36
"Radiovision," 22
Ratings, 83–85, *83*
RCA (Radio Corporation of America)
  color television, 40–41
  early television costs, 37–38
  patent challenge, 31–32
  Sarnoff, David, 27–28
  World's Fair exhibit, 35, 36
Recording, 62–63, *80*, 80–81
Reel-to-reel videotape recorders, 62–63
Remote controls, 48–51, *49*
Rentals, videocassette, 66
Roosevelt, Franklin D., 36
Rosing, Boris, 25
Ross, Steve, 69

S

Sales
  early television sets, 37–38
  VCRs, 65–66
Sarnoff, David
  broadcasting plan, 33
  color television, 40–41
  Farnsworth, Philo, work of, 29–31
  patent challenge, 31–32
  television's contribution to society, 38
  World's Fair exhibit, 36
  Zworykin, Vladimir, work of, 27–28
Satellites and satellite TV, *12*, 55–56, *56*, 59–60
Screens
  aspect ratio, 73–74, 76–77, *76*
  interactive, 98
  resolution, 73, 77
  scanning types, 78
Sedentary lifestyle, 48

Selenium, 19–20
Self-regulation, industry, 47–48, 83–85
Shutter glasses, 90–91
Signal transmission
    amplified radio signals, 18–19
    antennas, *54*
    cable television, 53–54
    radio, 18–19
    standards, 72–74
    telegraphy, 16–17
Social issues, 14–15, 38, 60–62
SONY, 63–65
Sony Corp. of America v. Universal City Studios,
    Inc., 64–65
Sound, 16–19, 81–82
Space Command, 50
Speakers, 81–82
Speech, freedom of, 84
Sports, *59*
Standards, industry, 38, 72–77
Stanton, Frank, *40*
Star Wars (movie), *95*
Stereotypes, 60
Streaming video, 70–71, *71*
Surround sound, 81–82
Swinton, A. A. Campbell, 25

T
Taped programming. *See* Videocassette recorders
Technology
    cathode ray tubes, 23–25
    closed-captioning, 65
    color television, 39–42
    digital television, 71–72
    digital video recorders, 80–81, *80*
    disk-based television, 19–23
    flatscreen televisions, 78–80, *79*
    gesture-controlled television, 86–88, *87, 88*
    high-definition television, 74–77
    history of improvements, 10–11
    holography, 94–96
    interactive television, 68–70, *69*, 96, 97–98, *97*
    organic light-emitting diode (OLED), 88–89
    remote controls, 48–51
    selenium cameras, 18
    sound transmission, 16–20
    3-D, 89–94, *91, 92*
    V-chip, 82–84, *83*
    videotape recording, 62–66

Telecommunications line installer and repairer, 47
Telecommunications Reform Act, 83
Telegraphy, 16–17, *17*
Telephones, 17
Television Decoder Circuitry Act, 65
Television repairpersons, 72
"Televisor," 20–22, *21*
Telstar, 55–56, *56*
Tesla, Nikola, 48–50
3-D technology, 89–94, *91, 92*
Tolman, Justin, 31
Transistors, 51, *51*
Transmission. *See* Signal transmission
TV Turnoff Week, 82
TV-Free America, 82

U
Ultrasonic remote controls, 50
U-Matic, 63
Universal City Studios, Inc., Sony Corp. of
    America v., 64–65

V
Vacuum tube technology, 18–19
V-chip technology, 82–84, *83*
VCRs (videocassette recorders), 62–66, *64*
VHS (Video Home System), 64
Video games, 66–67, *67, 87*
Video Home System (VHS), 64
Video stores, 66
Videocassette recorders (VCRs), 62–66, *64*
Viewership, 10
Vision, 20, *93*

W
Walson, John, 43, 54
Warner Communications, 68–70
Westinghouse Research Laboratory, 25–26
Wii, Nintendo, 67, *87*
Wireless radio waves, 17–19
Wireless remote controls, 49–51
World War II, 38–39
World's Fair, 35, 36

X
XBox 360 Kinect, 67

Z
Zenith Electronics Corporation, 50
Zworykin, Vladimir, 25–28, *27*, 29–31

PICTURE CREDITS

Cover: Victor Gmyria/Shutterstock.com
AP Images, 8, 40, 46, 59, 69, 75, 83
© Bettmann/Corbis, 27, 30, 54, 56, 61, 67
© Bruce McGowan/Alamy, 97
© Enigma/Alamy, 80
Gale, Cengage Learning, 24, 41, 57, 76, 88
© H. Armstrong Roberts/ClassicStock/
    Corbis, 11, 34
© Interfoto/Alamy, 9, 26
© Kristoffer Tripplaar/Alamy, 12
Library of Congress, 8
© Liquid Light/Alamy, 79
© Mary Evans Picture Library/Alamy, 49

© NetPics/Alamy, 9
© Paul Brown/Alamy, 64
© Philippe Lissac/Godong/Corbis, 87
© Photos 12/Alamy, 91, 95
© Richard Levine/Alamy, 92
© Robert Stainforth/Alamy, 71
© Rob James/Alamy, 73
© Sam P.S. II/Alamy, 9
© sciencephotos/Alamy, 51
SSPL/Getty Images, 21
© The Print Collector/Alamy, 17
© Underwood & Underwood/
    Corbis, 37

John Grabowski is a native of Brooklyn, New York. He holds a bachelor's degree in psychology from City College of New York and a master's degree in educational psychology from Teachers College, Columbia University. He was a teacher for thirty-nine years, as well as a freelance writer, specializing in the fields of sports, education, and comedy. His published works include fifty-three books; a nationally syndicated sports column; and articles for newspapers, magazines, and the programs of professional sports teams. He has also consulted on several math textbooks and written comedy for Jay Leno, Joan Rivers, Yakov Smirnoff, and numerous other comics. He and his wife, Patricia, live in Staten Island, New York, with their daughter, Elizabeth.